GOLD

B2 First

NEW EDITION

T0346278

CONTENTS

Introduction to the Gold B2 First Exam Maximiser

The **Gold B2 First Exam Maximiser** is specially designed to maximise your chances of success in the Cambridge English Qualifications: B2 First examination.

The **Exam Maximiser** will help you prepare for the Cambridge English Qualifications: B2 First exam by offering you:

- further **practice and revision** of all the important vocabulary, grammar and skills (reading, writing, listening and speaking) that you study in the Gold B2 First Coursebook.
- more **information about the kinds of questions** you will have to answer in the Cambridge English Qualifications: B2 First exam.
- guidance with the **strategies and techniques** you should use to tackle exam tasks.
- **exam-style exercises** so that you can practise using the techniques.
- regular **extra Use of English sections** to help you practise the language and strategies you have learnt.
- details of **Common errors** in the Cambridge English Qualifications: B2 First exam and how to avoid them.
- a complete **Practice exam** which you can use for preparation just before you sit the exam. This means that you will know exactly what to expect in each paper and that there are no unpleasant surprises.

How can I use the Gold B2 First Exam Maximiser?

The **Exam Maximiser** is very flexible and can be used by students in a variety of situations and in a variety of ways. Here are some typical situations:

> **1**
> You are doing a Cambridge English Qualifications: B2 First course with other students, probably over an academic year. You are all planning to take the exam at the same time.

You are using the **Gold B2 First Coursebook** in class. Sometimes you will also do the related exercises or even a whole unit from the **Exam Maximiser** in class, though your teacher will ask you to do exercises from it at home as well. You will use the entire **Exam Maximiser** or you will use it selectively, depending on your needs and the time available.

> **2**
> You have already done a Cambridge English Qualifications: B2 First course and you are now doing an intensive course to prepare for the exam.

Since you have already worked though the **Gold B2 First Coursebook** or perhaps another Cambridge English Qualifications: B2 First coursebook, you will use the **Exam Maximiser** in class. This, together with the **Practice Tests Plus Cambridge First 2 New Edition (2014)**, will give you a concentrated and highly focused short exam course.

> **3**
> You have a very short time in which to prepare for the Cambridge English Qualifications: B2 First exam.

Your level of English is already nearing Cambridge English Qualifications: B2 First exam standard, though you have not been following a coursebook. You now need exam skills. You will use the **Exam Maximiser** independently, without a coursebook, because you need practice in the exam tasks and how to approach them.

> **4**
> You are retaking the Cambridge English Qualifications: B2 First exam as unfortunately you were not successful in your first attempt.

You may be retaking the exam because you were not sufficiently familiar with the exam requirements. You will not need to follow a coursebook, but you will use the **Exam Maximiser** to develop your exam techniques and build up your confidence.

> **5**
> You are preparing for the exam on your own.

Maybe you are not attending a Cambridge English Qualifications: B2 First class, but wish to take the exam and prepare for it independently. You will get practice and preparation by using the **Exam Maximiser** by itself. You can give yourself additional practice by using the **Practice Tests Plus Cambridge First 2 New Edition (2014)** just before taking the exam.

What is in each unit?

The Exam Maximiser follows the structure of the Gold B2 First Coursebook and each unit provides further work on the language, skills and exam strategies you looked at in the Coursebook unit.

Each unit contains **Vocabulary** sections. These practise the words and expressions which you studied in the Gold B2 First Coursebook and introduce you to some new words and expressions as well. There are plenty of exercises to do, including exam-style tasks from the Reading and Use of English paper and crosswords and wordsearch grids for some fun.

You will find two **Grammar** sections in each unit. By doing the exercises in these sections, you can practise and revise the grammar points you have studied in the Gold B2 First Coursebook. Once again, there are exam-style tasks from the Reading and Use of English paper.

There is a **Speaking** section in every unit to work on language and strategies to help you do well in the Speaking exam. In these sections, you listen to or read examples of candidates performing the speaking tasks and complete the activities to develop your own speaking skills.

Every unit has a **Listening** section. These sections help you train for each of the four parts in the Listening paper. First, you read some information about the paper and are given some advice on the strategy you should use in that particular part. You do an exercise to help you practise the strategy and then an exam-style listening task. The tasks get more difficult as you move through the units in the Exam Maximiser, so that by the end of the book they are at the same level as the exam.

There is also a **Reading** section in each unit. Like the Listening sections, these provide you with information about the exam and strategies to use in each of the three parts of the Reading paper. You do some exercises to help you with the strategy and then you do an exam-style task. There is a vocabulary activity at the end of most Reading sections as well, so that you can practise dealing with unfamiliar words and phrases. Like the Listening sections, the Reading sections are easier at the beginning of the book, but are at the level of the exam at the end.

At the end of each unit you will find a **Writing** section. Again, you are given information about the exam and the kinds of writing tasks you have to do in Parts 1 and 2 of the Writing paper. You are also given a strategy to follow and then have an opportunity to put it into practice by doing some exercises, often using sample answers. You write your answers to these exercises in the Exam Maximiser. Finally, you look at an exam task and write your own answer to this task.

As well as the **Use of English** section in each unit, there are also **Use of English** sections in exam format after every two units. These provide practice in the tasks and are based on the topic areas of the two units, giving you the opportunity to review the vocabulary you have learnt.

At the back of the book, there is a section giving examples of **Common errors: B2 First** for each paper. There is also a short section on common language errors.

Once you have worked through all the units, you will be ready to try the **Practice exam** at the back of the book. Then you'll be really well prepared for the Cambridge English Qualifications: B2 First exam.

Good luck!

1 Bands and fans

Vocabulary
free-time activities

1 Find ten words in the wordsearch connected with music, bands, fans and leisure.

o	t	k	j	i	n	s	t	r	u	m	e	n	t
p	e	r	f	o	r	m	a	n	c	e	o	k	d
q	u	e	h	i	n	s	t	r	r	m	g	n	r
a	u	d	i	e	n	c	e	u	m	f	a	l	u
g	j	c	l	u	b	b	i	n	g	u	m	y	m
i	u	g	b	v	m	u	s	i	c	a	e	o	m
g	k	n	k	y	u	w	i	p	u	m	s	g	e
s	x	p	k	c	o	n	c	e	r	t	r	a	r

2 Find and correct the mistakes with collocations in sentences 1–8.

1 I really think listening music is relaxing.

2 Can you play at a musical instrument?

3 I try to go as many live concerts as possible – they're great!

4 I watch at television in the evenings after work.

5 It's much easier if I can make the shopping at the weekends.

6 I tend stay at home on Sundays.

7 Making yoga helps me switch off from problems at work.

8 I'm really in rock music – I love the strong beat.

Speaking
listening to and answering questions (Part 1)
▶ CB page 7

1 ▶ 01 Listen to the questions an examiner asks. Match questions 1–7 to answers A–I. There are two answers you do not need to use.

A My older brother actually. I can talk to him about almost anything.

B It's hard to say but I hope I'll be working as a doctor. I've just started at uni.

C All kinds really. Hip hop, rock, jazz. I really like classical music too.

D I play the violin.

E Yes, a brother and a sister. My brother is three years older than me and my sister is a year younger.

F We usually go to the seaside, but this year we're going to visit my brother in Madrid. He's studying there.

G The people. The town itself is very beautiful with a cathedral and a wonderful square, but it's the people that make it special.

H I was studying at school.

I English! I liked the science subjects too but English is my favourite.

About the exam:
In the Speaking test, Part 1, you and your partner are each asked one or two questions, and you give personal information and opinions.

Strategy:
- Give interesting answers but don't say so much that you dominate the conversation.
- Make sure your answers are quite short.

Reading
Gapped text (Part 6)
▶ CB page 8

About the exam:

In the Reading and Use of English paper, Part 6, you read a text with missing sentences. The sentences are after the text in jumbled order. You decide where they go in the text. There is always one extra sentence.

Strategy:

- Read the whole text first and make sure you understand it.
- Look at the words like pronouns (e.g. *it, she*), demonstratives (e.g. *this, that*) and possessive adjectives (*her, their*) in the sentences that have been removed from the text and decide what they refer to.
- When you have chosen the missing sentences, read the whole text through again with the sentences in place to make sure that it all makes sense.

1 You are going to read a newspaper article about writing pop songs. Read the article and decide which of the titles 1 or 2 summarises the article best.

1 The science of the pop song

2 How writing songs has changed

2 Six sentences have been removed from the article. Choose from sentences A–G the one which fits each gap (1–6). There is one extra sentence you do not need to use.

A Even he can't account for the song's success but it certainly shows that pop doesn't always have to be manufactured and designed by a committee.

B One way record companies manage to do this is by including producers as part of song-writing teams.

C But somewhere along the line that all changed.

D You will see that huge teams of people are involved in its creation.

E Instead of gathering in a recording studio, they collaborate through file sharing.

F It rarely involved more than two people, one to write lyrics, the other to set them to music.

G It then took them only 12 minutes to actually write the song.

Writing a successful pop song might not seem too complicated at first glance. After all, it just takes two or three short verses, repeated choruses, a couple of hooks and a good melody, all wrapped up in about three minutes. But just take a look at the credits for any typical contemporary hit. **1** One recent number-one single was the result of the work of five writers, two producers and a remixer. The current top ten **features** forty different writers and nineteen producers. Nowadays, it certainly seems to be a case of the more the merrier.

For most of the 20th Century, song writing was a very different process. **2** Singer-songwriters like Bob Dylan became famous for writing and performing entirely on their own. So how did we end up with songs that have as many as five composers, two of whom might not even have been in the room while the song was being written? One contributing factor has been sampling and the way it makes constructing new tracks out of old ones seem legitimate.

But are the new tracks really new? Pop songs almost always have the same verse-chorus structure, and a rhythmic pattern of four beats to the bar that almost never **varies**. Somehow pop still manages to convince us of its own novelty. **3** They contribute hooks, sound effects and technological innovations of various kinds to conceal the fact that we are actually hearing the same five or six chord progressions known to appeal to listeners.

Of course, digital technology has made it easier for the work of different producers and writers to be combined. **4** The original version of one successful hit was released in Hawaii in 2012, but then **radically** remixed by a German DJ in 2014 before it went on to become a chart success. This can still be an expensive business though.

In 2011, National Public Radio in the USA tried to work out just how much it costs to produce a typical pop song by analysing a recent chart contender. They **established** that $53,000 was spent in advance just bringing the four writers and producers together. **5** Nevertheless, the final budget for recording and marketing came to over a million dollars. The single actually **flopped**, only reaching 59 in the U.S. charts.

Perhaps a failure like that serves to remind us that songwriting is not a science and nobody is really certain what makes a hit. In the end, what connects a song with the public consciousness and gives it a life of its own just cannot be calculated or predicted. One recent example is the 2014 global hit written and performed by the then unknown Irish singer-songwriter Hozier, and recorded in the attic of his parent's house. **6** Sometimes, it just takes a bit of magic.

3 Look at verbs 1–3 from the article in Activity 2 and cross out the words in italics that cannot be used with them.

1 make *something easier/your homework/a hit/a friend*
2 record *a song/your answers/a dish/a message*
3 become *famous/a teacher/a baby/an adult*

4 Choose the definition, A or B, that matches the meaning of words 1–5. Check the words in bold in context in the article.

1 features
   A includes   B highlights
2 varies
   A changes   B disagrees
3 radically
   A badly   B completely
4 established
   A started   B found out
5 flopped
   A fell down   B failed to succeed

5 Find words in the article to match definitions 1–4.

1 the words of a song
2 songs or pieces of music on a record or CD
3 the main rhythm that a piece of music has
4 passages or phrases used in popular music to make songs attractive or interesting to listeners

6 Look at sentences 1–3 from the article. Choose the sentence, A or B, that is closest in meaning to the original. Look at the article again and use the whole context to help you.

1 So how did we end up with songs that have as many as five composers, two of whom might not even have been in the room while the song was being written?
   A How has it become possible for songs to have so many composers, some of whom were not physically present when the song was being written?
   B Why are songs sometimes finished off by more composers than those who started to write them?

2 The original version of one successful hit was released in Hawaii in 2012, but then radically remixed by a German DJ in 2014 before it went on to become a chart success.
   A In 2014 a German DJ made a lot of money by copying a song that had been a hit in Hawaii in 2012.
   B The song became a hit in 2014 after a German DJ changed the original recording that had been made in Hawaii in 2012.

3 Sometimes, it just takes a bit of magic.
   A Sometimes, it's better to only use a small amount of magic.
   B Sometimes, a small amount of magic is all that is necessary.

7 Read the complete article again. Which of the opinions do you agree with? Think of three reasons you would give for your opinions.

Technology has really helped to make pop music more exciting.

The singer-songwriters of the past were far more talented than modern pop stars.

There's no such thing as originality in pop music.

Grammar
simple and continuous forms in the present and present habit
▶ CB page 10

1 Choose the correct option in italics to complete the sentences.

1 I *have/am having* a ticket for the concert on Friday and I *get/am getting* really excited!
2 The group *come/are coming* from the same school as I went to, which makes it even more exciting.
3 They *perform/are performing* all over Europe now, or at least that's what my friend *tells/is telling* me.
4 I *understand/am understanding* that the concert is sold out. I can't wait to *hear/be hearing* them play!
5 I *know/am knowing* one of the roadies and at the moment he *works/is working* backstage on some of their gigs here in the UK.
6 He *says/is saying* that the band *are really looking forward/really look forward* to coming back to their home town to play on Friday.
7 Their fans *love/are loving* them wherever they *play/are playing*, but we're special for them.
8 On their latest album they *sound/are sounding* more like Coldplay but I *like/am liking* it a lot.
9 Some people *criticise/are criticising* them for that, but I *disagree/am disagreeing*. I'm still their biggest fan.
10 The sound at live gigs is so loud – it's very hard to *get used to/getting used to*.

Use of English
Multiple-choice cloze (Part 1)
▶ CB page 11

About the exam:
In the Reading and Use of English paper, Part 1, you read a text with eight gaps and choose the best word from four options to fit each gap. The correct word may be: part of a fixed phrase or collocation, part of a phrasal verb, the only word that makes sense in the sentence (e.g. a connector), the word that fits with the word(s) before or after the gap.

Strategy:
- Read the title and the whole text without worrying about the gaps so that you understand what it is about.
- Go through the text, stopping at each gap. Read the four options.
- Check the words before and after the gap. Then choose the best option.

1 **For questions 1–8, read the text below and decide which word (A, B, C or D) best fits each gap. There is an example at the beginning (0).**

Music on your mind

You know the feeling – you're listening to music and suddenly your whole **(0)** _A mood_ changes from sad to happy. This mind-altering power of music is amazing, and internet music sites are using sophisticated ways of **(1)** .... us in touch with new artists. They monitor our online searches or online listening habits **(2)** .... patterns, and the results are often surprising – would you believe that AC/DC fans may well enjoy Beethoven?

Musicians have been **(3)** .... unforgettable music for centuries, using accepted ideas about the emotional appeal of certain combinations of musical sounds. It's **(4)** .... knowledge that major chords sound upbeat **(5)** .... minor chords sound mournful – in tests, even children as young as three connect music in major keys to happy faces. Scientists investigating the subject have been **(6)** .... various experiments such as scanning the brains of people while they listen to music. One thing they **(7)** .... across is that music triggers activity in the motor regions of the brain, which could explain why we often need to **(8)** .... our feet to music. The possibilities for medicine and business are exciting!

0	**A** mood	**B** atmosphere	**C** temper	**D** idea
1	**A** placing	**B** putting	**C** making	**D** doing
2	**A** looking out	**B** looking for	**C** looking up	**D** looking after
3	**A** constructing	**B** forming	**C** inventing	**D** composing
4	**A** great	**B** usual	**C** common	**D** wide
5	**A** while	**B** during	**C** since	**D** so
6	**A** taking	**B** making	**C** doing	**D** having
7	**A** came	**B** went	**C** brought	**D** took
8	**A** tap	**B** bang	**C** hit	**D** strike

2 **Look at the answers to Activity 1 again. Underline:**
1 two phrasal verbs.
2 three collocations.
3 one fixed phrase.

Listening
Multiple matching (Part 3)
▶ CB page 12

About the exam:
In the Listening paper, Part 3, you read eight statements or questions and hear five different people speaking about the same topic. You match each speaker to the appropriate statement or question. There are three extra statements or questions you do not need to use. You hear all the speakers twice.

Strategy:
- Read the instructions and the questions or statements carefully.
- Underline the key words in the statements. Then listen for these key ideas when you hear the speakers the first time.
- When you hear the speakers the second time, decide on the correct answer.
- At the end, check that you have only used each statement or question once.

1 ▶ **02 You will hear five different people talking about a live pop concert they have been to. Choose from the list (A–H) what each speaker disliked most about the concert. Use each letter only once. There are three extra letters which you do not need to use.**

A   The type of music played
B   The arena and the stage   Speaker 1 ☐
C   The location of the concert   Speaker 2 ☐
D   The audience participation   Speaker 3 ☐
E   The quality of the sound   Speaker 4 ☐
F   The price of the tickets   Speaker 5 ☐
G   The facilities at the venue
H   The long wait to get in

Grammar

used to and *would* for past habit

▶ CB page 13

1 Read the extracts about music and cross out the incorrect verb form in italics.

1 Throughout history, people *would/did/used to* make sure their children had classical music lessons from a young age. Some parents *did/had used to do/used to do* this because they thought it was good for mental discipline. Others *believed/used to believe/would believe* that knowledge of important works of classical music was part of a good general education.

2 As soon as films were invented, accompanying music became important. In the early days of silent films, cinemas *did/would/used to* hire a professional musician to play the piano or organ. This pianist *would/got used to/used to* sit at the front of the cinema and play whatever music he/she thought was suitable – customers *would/were used to/got used to* hearing different kinds of music in every cinema. Once sound was introduced, things became more consistent, and classical music has long been a favourite choice. Classical music has regularly featured in pop culture, and has often been used as background music for movies, television programmes and advertisements. As a result, avid fans of popular music *are used to/would/have got used to* regularly hearing classical music although they may not have recognised it as such.

2 Sentences 1–6 below each have a word missing. Complete the sentences with the words in the box.

get	got	to (x2)	used	would

1 When I was a child I used hate classical music, but I loved rock.

2 Every time I went to a concert I buy a T-shirt to remind me of it.

3 My brothers to go to football matches instead of coming to rock concerts with me.

4 After a while I used to going to music events on my own.

5 My mother could not used to me doing different things from my brothers.

6 Now I think she's got used it.

Use of English

Key word transformation (Part 4)

About the exam:

In the Reading and Use of English paper, Part 4, there are six unconnected sentences. For each one you complete a new sentence so that it has a similar meaning, using a word given in bold. You must not change this word. This part tests a range of grammatical structures and vocabulary.

Strategy:
- Don't change the key word.
- Only write between two and five words, including the given word. Contractions (e.g. *won't*) count as two words.

1 Complete the second sentence so that it has a similar meaning to the first sentence, using the word given. Do not change the word given. You must use between two and five words, including the word given.

0 I decided not to learn to play the piano as it seemed very difficult.

UP

I decided not to take up learning to play the piano because it seemed very difficult.

1 I lived in London as a child, but now I live in Paris.

USED

I live in Paris now, but _____ London as a child.

2 When I lived in London, I went to the music shop on the corner every Saturday.

WOULD

Every Saturday _____ the music shop on the corner when I lived in London.

3 It's become easy for me to sing live as I do it so much.

GOT

I've _____ as I do it so much.

4 I find watching TV quite relaxing in the evenings.

FEEL

Watching TV _____ in the evenings.

5 I don't go to live concerts very often.

HARDLY

I _____ live concerts.

6 I only found your message by chance when I was looking for something else.

ACROSS

I only _____ accident when I was looking for something else.

Writing
Informal email (Part 2)
▶ CB page 14

About the exam:

In Part 2 of the Writing paper you may have the opportunity to write a letter or email. You will be given part of a letter or email to reply to, and you should write 140–190 words. The letter or email may be semi-formal or informal.

Strategy:

Read the instructions and the whole task very carefully. Identify:
- who you are writing to.
- why you are writing.
- what you have to write about.
- whether you need to use a semi-formal or informal style.

You will probably need to use functions such as explaining, giving information, suggesting. Make sure you cover all the points mentioned in the email or letter in the task.

1 Look at the task and decide if statements 1–5 below are true (T) or false (F).

> You have received an email from your English-speaking friend, Julia.
>
> From: Julia
> Subject: Music Club
>
> I'm going to start a music club here! I want to play music from all over the world, and I'd like to visit your country to get ideas. When's the best time to come? What's the best way to find out what kind of music young people like?
> Can you recommend some local music clubs I could visit?
>
> Reply soon,
> Julia

1 You should write in a formal style.
2 Your reply should provide various kinds of information.
3 You have to ask some questions.
4 You can use abbreviations and smileys in your answer.
5 You should write 140–190 words.

2 Write your email for the task. You must use grammatically correct sentences with accurate spelling and punctuation in an appropriate style.

3 Match the sentences below to the functions in the box. You can use two of the functions more than once.

> explaining   inviting   making offers
> making suggestions   refusing an invitation
> stating preferences

1 What I'd rather do is go to the evening performance.
2 I'm afraid I won't be able to make it in November.
3 Maybe we could meet outside the box office at seven.
4 The thing is, the venue's a difficult place to find so it's better to go together.
5 I'm going to a gig tonight – do you fancy coming along?
6 July is the best month for festivals so that would be a really good time to come.
7 Would you like me to buy the tickets?
8 Unfortunately, that's when I have some of my exams.

4 Look at the task below. Then read the email the student has written and do the following.

- Identify any missing information.
- Underline any sentences that are too formal.
- Correct any language mistakes.

> You have received this email from your English-speaking friend, Jo.
>
> From: Jo
> Subject: Next week
>
> Hi Inga – I'm really looking forward to coming to stay with you next week. If you can't meet me at the station at 3, I'll get a taxi.
>
> Tell me about the music festival we're going to! Do I need to bring anything special?
>
> See you soon!
>
> Jo

> Hi Jo,
>
> I'm looking forward to see you, too! I am sorry to inform you that I am unable to meet you at the station. I'll be in college then and I can't missing it because I've got exams soon. The other bad news is that there isn't any taxis at our station, but there is a very good bus service – every 10 minutes, and it's better because it's a lot cheaper! Get the number 18 and get off at the post office – you know how to walking to my house from there. Good news about the festival – I've got front-row tickets! There are loads of great bands and we'll have a lot of fun. It's in the local football stadium, so there'll be lots of people there.
>
> That's all for now – see you next week.
>
> Yours sincerely,
> Inga

2 Relative values

Vocabulary
formation of adjectives
▶ CB page 17

1 Look at the adjectives of feeling in the box. Which five are negative?

confusing	depressing	encouraging	frustrating	harmful
imaginative	independent	irritated	practical	relaxed

2 Complete sentences 1–6 with a suitable adjective from Activity 1.

1 She found the lecture very .... and couldn't understand her own notes afterwards.
2 She's a very .... person who likes to do things on her own.
3 I feel most .... when I'm sitting outside in the sun.
4 When newspapers write stories about celebrities that are not true, it can be .... to their careers.
5 Too much rain can be rather .... when you want to have a picnic!
6 I get very .... by people who talk loudly on mobile phones in public.

3 Complete the paragraph about Jamie with the adjective form of the words in the box.

create	emotion	pessimist	real	reliability	social
sympathy	thought				

Jamie is a very **(1)** .... person. He always seems to see the negative side of everything. He can be quite **(2)** .... and gets upset if he is criticised, but this does not affect his work. In his work he is **(3)** .... and puts forward lots of unusual and interesting ideas. He gets on well with colleagues and is very **(4)** .... , often inviting them to evenings out. Colleagues describe him as **(5)** .... towards people in difficulty, always prepared to spend time with them and offer advice. He is able to set **(6)** .... targets which are possible to achieve. He is always **(7)** .... when meeting deadlines and he never lets others down. He brings a **(8)** .... approach to his work, never jumping in too quickly and making mistakes.

Use of English
Word formation (Part 3)
▶ CB page 17

About the exam:
In the Reading and Use of English paper, Part 3, you read a text with a gap in some of the lines. You change the word in capitals at the end of these lines to fit the gap.

Strategy:
- Read the title and the whole text to make sure you understand it.
- Look at each sentence in detail. Check:
  - what kind of word you need (noun, verb, adjective, adverb).
  - whether you need to add a negative prefix or suffix.
  - whether the word needs to be plural.

1 For questions 1–8, read the text below. Use the word given in capitals at the end of some of the lines to form a word that fits in the gap in the same line. There is an example at the beginning (0).

Gossip is good for you!

Gossip has a bad name. Many people say it is
(0) _unkind_ and others claim that it is often   **KIND**
(1) .... and therefore a waste of time. Talking   **ACCURATE**
about someone behind their back can cause
(2) .... to break down and create great   **RELATE**
(3) .... But can it have a positive function as   **HAPPY**
well? The most popular television programmes
are soap operas which often have rather
(4) .... storylines in which strange characters   **DEPRESS**
indulge in creating and circulating **(5)** .... and   **PLEASE**
vicious rumours that in the real world would be
(6) .... – and yet we all take great delight in   **ACCEPT**
discussing the ups and downs of their lives.
Why is this? Could it be that they give us an
alternative family which we can gossip about
without **(7)** .... creating trouble? Taking an   **ACTUAL**
interest in other people is considered to be a
(8) .... activity in some circles – it gives the   **HEALTH**
feeling of being informed about what's
happening in the wider world. So gossiping
may be good for us after all!

Reading
Multiple matching (Part 7)
▶ CB page 18

About the exam:
In the Reading and Use of English paper, Part 7, you match questions or statements to several short texts.

Strategy:
- Read the text through quickly to get a general idea of what it is about.
- Underline key words and phrases in the questions.
- Find expressions in the text that have a similar meaning to the key words.

1 You are going to read a magazine article about people who discovered they had a relative they didn't know about. Read the texts on page 14 quickly and decide if the statements are true (T) or false (F).

1 All the people are unhappy about what happened to them.

2 All the people only met recently.

2 For questions 1–10, choose from the sections (A–D). The key words and expressions have been underlined for you. The sections may be chosen more than once.

Which two people

live near one another?   **1** ☐

do the same work?   **2** ☐

met thanks to someone else?   **3** ☐

blame someone else for what happened to them?   **4** ☐

plan to meet for the first time soon?   **5** ☐

had a good relationship before they found out the truth?   **6** ☐

were not equally knowledgeable about their family history?   **7** ☐

plan to publish something about their experience?   **8** ☐

were at the same event when they were very young?   **9** ☐

were the victims of a cruel experiment?   **10** ☐

Finding family

Ever wondered if you had a relative you knew nothing about? It's not as rare as you might think.

A Harry and Samuel Quintana

Harry Quintana and his cousin Samuel have a lot in common, even if they didn't know that until they met again recently after fifty years. Samuel grew up in South Africa and only visited the USA, where his cousin Harry lived, once as a very small child. Both children attended a family wedding. After that neither boy's parents talked about their relatives overseas. As a result, the cousins grew up on different sides of the Atlantic Ocean, unaware of each other and the parallel lives they were leading. Harry Quintana graduated in dentistry and decided to specialise in the treatment of children. Until he saw Samuel's name in a conference programme, he had no idea that over in South Africa his cousin had already become well established in exactly the same profession. When the cousins met recently they found out they like the same foods and have both recently taken up golf.

B Carlos Rodriquez and Juan García

When Juan García moved to a new neighbourhood at the age of thirteen, a classmate introduced him to Carlos Rodriquez, who lived in the next street. They were so similar in looks and interests that they were jokingly known as the twins. However, ten years into their friendship, Juan and Carlos were stunned to learn that they are siblings. Juan had always known that he was adopted as a baby but he didn't search for his birth parents until he was twenty-one. It was then that he discovered his biological father shared Carlos's father's surname. A DNA test confirmed that they are indeed related. When the test results came through, Juan and Carlos were both shocked but delighted. Juan remarked, 'I was raised as an only child and always longed for brothers and sisters. Now I'm lucky enough for my best friend to be my brother!'

C Petra Holmes and Elisa Manning

Petra Holmes and Elisa Manning have lived very similar lives. Both born in New York, they edited their high school newspapers and studied the same thing at university. It was only at the age of thirty-five that they discovered each other and just how similar they were: identical twins who had been separated as babies and gone to live with new families as part of a scientific study of child development.

The truth came out when Elisa decided to try to trace her birth mother. She was able to look at the records and saw that she had an identical twin, Petra. When she finally found her sister, they put the pieces of the story together. 'Nature intended for us to grow up together, so we think it is a crime we were separated,' said Elisa. They have taken this up with the psychologist responsible, but according to the twins he didn't even apologise. The sisters are working on a book about their experience.

D Brenda McLaughlin and Allison Burroughs

Brenda McLaughlin had spent years compiling an extensive family tree in which she had recorded all her father's relatives' names along with the dates they were born, when they married and when they died. Brenda, who lives in Sydney, Australia, knew about their various offspring, including the children of her father's youngest cousin, Irene. Meanwhile, Allison Burroughs, Irene's daughter, was living on the other side of the country in Perth. Although Brenda knew about her and her younger brother, there had been no contact. Then, out of the blue, she received an email from Allison, who had also been looking into the McLaughlin family and had found Brenda's name on a website devoted to genealogy. Allison knew virtually nothing about the family and was amazed and delighted with Brenda's research.

'We've set up a family reunion next Christmas,' says Brenda. 'Better late than never is what I say.'

---

3 **Find phrasal verbs in the texts A–D in Activity 2 with the same meanings as the underlined words and phrases in sentences 1–8 below.**

1 William <u>discovered</u> that the person he had thought was his uncle was actually not related to him at all. (Text A)

2 I've just <u>started doing</u> yoga. I love it. (Text A)

3 When her exam results <u>arrived</u> she was overjoyed to see that she had passed everything. (Text B)

4 Tamara had always <u>wanted</u> a cat and now she had one – a gorgeous black kitten. (Text B)

5 Finally, the real reason Tom had run away from home <u>emerged</u>. He had always hated his stepfather. (Text C)

6 The student representative has <u>raised</u> the issue of access to the computer room with the school director. (Text C)

7 I've been <u>investigating</u> ways of getting from Barcelona to Montpellier and the train seems the best option. (Text D)

8 It's good to <u>organise</u> frequent meetings between family members. (Text D)

Grammar
adverbs and extreme adjectives
▶ CB page 20

1 **Find and correct the mistakes with adverbs in sentences 1–8 below. There are four mistakes.**

1 We followed her directions as close as we could, but we still got lost on the way to the farm.

2 In the afternoons we were free to do whatever we liked.

3 She handed in her essay too lately and the teacher refused to mark it.

4 As hardly as I try, I can never manage to remember all my relatives' birthdays.

5 I'm not as close to my sister as I am to my brother.

6 She spent her money so free that at the end of the month she had nothing left.

7 I've been seeing a lot of Alicia lately. We've become really good friends.

8 It's strange that we get on so well because we have hardly anything in common.

2 **Complete sentences 1–8 below with an appropriate adjective from the box. You do not need to use all the adjectives.**

angry   big   brilliant   difficult
exhausted   enormous   frightened
furious   impossible   intelligent
terrified   tired

1 The test was really _____ and most of the students got low marks.

2 Max is certainly very clever but his brother Albert is absolutely _____ .

3 I'm a bit _____ with Tim. He completely forgot my birthday.

4 We really wanted to meet up but it was completely _____ in the end.

5 I'm going to have an early night. I'm absolutely _____ .

6 She was very _____ of dogs when she was a child, but now she loves them.

7 Fauzia's new house is absolutely _____ ! It's got so much more space than her last place.

8 If you're really _____ , a coffee might help.

Listening
Multiple choice (Part 4)
▶ CB page 21

About the exam:
In the Listening paper, Part 4, you hear an interview/discussion between two people. You answer questions with three options to choose from. You have one minute to read the questions.

Strategy:
• Read the questions and the three options.
• The first time you listen, underline any key words you hear and mark the possible answers.
• The second time you listen, check your answers.

1 ▶ 03 **You will hear an interview with a young singer and dancer called Susie Tomkins, talking about her relationships and her career. For questions 1–7, choose the best answer (A, B or C).**

1 How does Susie feel about her family?
  A grateful for their constant support
  B convinced that her talent came from them
  C pleased that they understood her ambitions

2 What does Susie say about her relationship with students at her first school?
  A She was upset by their attitude towards her.
  B She found it hard to share their interests.
  C She understood the depth of their feelings.

3 How does Susie feel about being in a musical show now?
  A She appreciates the effect she has on people.
  B She looks forward to meeting fans afterwards.
  C She finds the experience unexpectedly challenging.

4 What does Susie say about the adult performers in the musical?
  A She found them easy to get on with.
  B She admired their professional approach.
  C She was glad of their assistance with practical things.

5 Susie values her relationship with her best friend because
  A it boosts her own confidence on stage.
  B it enables her to talk about problems openly.
  C it gives her insights into the entertainment world.

6 How does Susie feel about her career choices so far?
  A sorry that she can't always live a normal life
  B regretful of missing time with friends
  C annoyed by the criticism of others

7 What is Susie's attitude towards theatrical awards?
  A She is proud of the achievement they represent.
  B She feels pressure after winning one of them.
  C She thinks they are generally over-valued.

Grammar
verb patterns: -ing or infinitive
▶ CB page 22

1 **Choose the correct alternative in italics to complete the sentences.**

1 I stopped running because *it was raining too hard/ I needed the exercise.*

2 I tried to write an email but *he wouldn't accept my apology/I couldn't think what to say.*

3 I remembered buying the milk *but I couldn't remember where I put it/so I put it in the fridge.*

4 I regret to tell you that *I am breaking up with you/ you have not got the job.*

2 **Complete sentences 1–6 with the correct form of the verbs in brackets.**

1 I started _____ when I was only three. (*dance*)

2 Do you ever regret _____ her about the problem? (*tell*)

3 Sadly, although I wanted _____ his friend, he didn't like me. (*be*)

4 I want _____ a new mobile phone, but what should I get? (*buy*)

5 I actually enjoy _____ to the cinema on my own. (*go*)

6 I can't stand _____ football – it's so boring! (*watch*)

3 **Find and correct the mistakes with -ing and infinitives in sentences 1–6. Tick the sentences that are correct.**

1 She made him help her do the cooking, but he wasn't very good at it!

2 I stopped to smoke over five years ago and now I feel great!

3 He tried to phone her number, but she didn't answer.

4 I'll never forget to see the royal wedding on television – it was beautiful.

5 I regret informing you that your application for the job has been unsuccessful.

6 I'm keen on doing as much sport as possible to keep fit.

Speaking
agreeing and disagreeing (Part 3)
▶ CB page 23

1 ▶ **04 Complete conversations 1 and 2 with the phrases in the boxes. Then listen and check.**

1

| Exactly! | I hadn't thought of that. | So do I. |
| I'm not sure about that. | What about you? | |

A: I think it's so important to get on well with your parents.

B: (1) _____ I have a great relationship with my folks. I think it's more important than getting on with your brothers and sisters.

A: Hmm. (2) _____ I mean, I think it's important to have a good relationship with them too.

B: It's much more difficult if you come from a very large family.

A: (3) _____ I guess it's almost inevitable that there will be someone you don't get along so well with if there are a lot of you.

B: (4) _____ There are five of us and though I get on fine with my older brother and with my two sisters, my younger brother and I just don't have anything in common. (5) _____

A: Well, I've only got one sister and I really enjoy doing things with her.

2

Good point.	Well, actually
I see what you mean	but I'm not convinced.
What's your view on that?	

A: I saw a programme about relationships last night that said that friends were more important than family.

B: I saw it too – but (6) _____ Certainly friends are pretty crucial – it'd be a poor social life without them! But family must always come first.

A: (7) _____ some things the programme said are certainly true for me. They said your friends have a lot more influence on you when you're young than your parents do. (8) _____

B: (9) _____ in my case it was the other way round. I learnt my values from my parents. I think it's their responsibility to teach you how to behave.

A: (10) _____ Parents do need to teach their children how to behave, but I think you can also learn from your friends.

Writing
Essay (Part 1) ▶ CB page 24

About the exam:

In Part 1 of the Writing paper, you have to write an essay for your teacher in 140–190 words. You will be given a topic and a question, and two ideas to write about. You must use both these ideas in your essay, and also add one idea of your own.

Strategy:

- Read the task carefully.
- Think of ways of expanding the notes you are given. Think of advantages and disadvantages of each one.
- Think of your own idea, with a reason.
- You should have an introduction that leads into the topic and a conclusion that answers the question.
- Use a semi-formal style.
- Include both the ideas in the task and your own idea.

1 Read the essay task and question below.

In your English class you have been talking about family life. Now, your teacher has asked you to write an essay.

Write an essay using all the notes and give reasons for your point of view.

> Every family is different in size. Do you think it is better to grow up in a large family or a small one?
>
> **Notes**
> Write about:
> 1 company
> 2 support
> 3 .... (your own idea)

2 Complete the sentences with the linking words in the box.

although	as	as well as	however
in spite of	whereas		

1 It's great to have lots of brothers and sisters .... you always have someone to spend time with.

2 If you have cousins living near you .... friends, you can talk to them about problems.

3 I was always close to my sister .... the big age gap between us.

4 Parents can always give you support. .... , grandparents have more time to listen to you.

5 It's good to have younger siblings, ... they can also be annoying!

6 A big family can be very noisy, ... a small family may be much quieter.

3 Look at the points a student wants to make in his/her essay. Which points are not relevant?

> 1 <u>company</u> big family: always someone to talk to/competitive/play games small family: quiet/boring/internet
>
> 2 <u>support</u> big family: siblings listen to problems/parents pay for everything/don't need friends
> small family: more independent/can live in a flat/can spend more money
>
> 3 <u>own point</u>: grandparents you can find out about the old days/they have time to listen to you/they don't understand modern life

4 Underline the linking words used to connect points with reasons.

> Is it better to live in a large or small family?
>
> This is a difficult question to answer as we can't choose our family, and every family is different. We can only experience our own family! However, there are points I can make.
>
> In a big family with lots of siblings there is always someone to talk to and listen to your problems because they know you well and can really help you. On the other hand, siblings can also be very competitive, and that can cause problems.
>
> The problem with a small family is that life can be very quiet, and possibly boring, even though it does teach people to be independent, which is a good thing. Nevertheless, they need to make lots of friends outside their family.
>
> It is a great advantage when grandparents live in the family as well, since they can teach you about life in the past. They also have more time to listen to you as they don't go out to work like parents do, but sometimes they have problems understanding modern technology.
>
> On balance, it seems that there is no right answer, but there are more advantages than disadvantages to living in a bigger family.

5 Read the task below. Follow the steps above.

In your English class you have been talking about family relationships. Now, your teacher has asked you to write an essay.

Write an essay using all the points and give reasons for your point of view.

> Is it better to be the oldest or the youngest in a family?
>
> **Notes**
> Write about:
> 1 time parents have with you
> 2 responsibilities you have
> 3 .... (your own idea)

6 Write your own answer to the task.

Multiple-choice cloze (Part 1)

For questions 1–8, read the text below and decide which answer (A, B, C or D) best fits each gap. There is an example at the beginning (0).

Rock 'n' roll drummers are as fit as sports stars

Bands are **(0)** *A, made up of* talented people, each with their own **(1)** .... and status within the group. But drummers are different.

Doctors monitored drummers during rehearsals and **(2)** .... performances and their findings were surprising. Many drummers are as fit as **(3)** .... athletes.

Good drumming requires a combination of physical and mental agility, and fitness is vital. **(4)** .... a performance a drummer can lose two litres of fluid and burn **(5)** .... hundreds of calories. One described it as having a three-hour workout every night. Modern drummers often follow a strict fitness regime, working with personal trainers and sticking to a special **(6)** .... Several hours before a performance, many start warming up by doing stretching exercises; like athletes, they eat bananas to **(7)** .... their energy levels and take specially prepared energy drinks with them **(8)** .... The comparison between drummers and sports stars seems fair.

0	**A** made up of	**B** put up with	**C** come up with	**D** done up with
1	**A** part	**B** purpose	**C** role	**D** section
2	**A** live	**B** realistic	**C** true	**D** authentic
3	**A** important	**B** special	**C** elite	**D** exclusive
4	**A** During	**B** While	**C** Through	**D** Whilst
5	**A** off	**B** out	**C** back .	**D** in
6	**A** nutrition	**B** menu	**C** diet	**D** food
7	**A** keep up	**B** take up	**C** get up	**D** give up
8	**A** at stage	**B** on stage	**C** in stage	**D** by stage

Open cloze (Part 2)

For questions 9–16, read the text below and think of the word which best fits each gap. Use only one word in each gap. There is an example at the beginning (0).

Mother, father or both?

In modern society men and women expect equality at work, but can this extend to **(0)** *bringing* up children? Is it realistic **(9)** .... expect new parents to share parenting, or are their roles already defined? **(10)** .... it is usually mothers who stay at home, many fathers **(11)** .... now asking for an equal opportunity to spend time **(12)** .... care of their children. The question is whether fathers can really **(13)** .... equal partners in childcare. It's possible that the biological advantage mothers have is impossible to overcome.

Many couples would like to share the responsibility of **(14)** .... after their children, but this can create financial difficulties. If both parents decide to work part-time, there will be a drop in income, and so one **(15)** .... other of the parents often chooses to return to full-time employment.

Of course there are parents who have managed to share childcare responsibilities, but often the mother feels guilty about giving **(16)** .... her role as the primary carer.

Maybe it's a case of trial and error in establishing the way forward.

Word formation (Part 3)

For questions 17–24, read the text below. Use the word given in capitals at the end of some of the lines to form a word that fits in the gap in the same line. There is an example at the beginning (0).

Music or architecture?

'Talking about music is like dancing about architecture.'

It is thought the **(0)** _composer_ Clara Schumann said this in 1846, although there's no conclusive **(17)** .... of that. But what did she mean? Let's think about it. Firstly, music sends its own message to its listeners, and so it may be **(18)** .... to talk about what it means. But it is not **(19)** .... to imagine a dance troupe doing an interesting and meaningful **(20)** .... with architecture as its topic. If so, Clara's **(21)** .... quote would be wrong and talking about music may be more **(22)** .... than she thought. People can hold their own **(23)** .... opinions about all forms of art, and the artist's own intention is not **(24)** .... any more valid than anyone else's interpretation of their work. So, let's keep talking about art, music and films. Wouldn't life be dull if no one wanted to share their opinion!

COMPOSE	
PROVE	
POINT	
POSSIBLE	
PERFORM	
ORIGIN	
USE	
PERSON	
NECESSARY	

Key word transformation (Part 4)

For questions 25–30, complete the second sentence so that it has a similar meaning to the first sentence, using the word given. Do not change the word given. You must use between two and five words, including the word given. Here is an example (0).

Example:

0 I am considering taking up golf.

OF

I _am thinking of_ taking up golf.

25 She was watching television but turned it off when her son arrived.

STOPPED

She .... when her son arrived.

26 I was cleaning the cupboard when I found an old diary.

CAME

I .... when I was cleaning the cupboard.

27 When I was young I enjoyed listening to rock music but now I prefer classical.

LISTEN

When I was young .... to rock music but now I prefer classical.

28 I always went on holiday with my family to France every summer.

WOULD

I .... on holiday with my family to France every summer.

29 I'm still working on that report.

FINISHED

I .... that report yet.

30 There's a good chance that my team will win the cup this year.

VERY

It .... my team will win the cup this year.

3 Things that matter

Vocabulary

money
▶ CB page 26

1 **Choose the correct option in italics to complete the sentences.**

1 It's a bad idea to lend money *to/for* a friend as it often causes problems.

2 It's nice when rich people give some money *away/down* to charity.

3 I'm always short *of/about* money at the end of the month.

4 It's important to try to live *within/about* your means and not borrow money from anyone.

5 I've just won a small amount of money and I feel as though I've got money *for/to* burn!

6 It's not easy to live *with/on* a tight budget but that's what students have to do.

2 **For questions 1–6, complete the second sentence so that it has a similar meaning to the first sentence, using the word given. Do not change the word given. You must use between two and five words, including the word given.**

1 She's incredibly rich so she can buy anything she likes.

BURN

She's .... so she can buy anything she likes.

2 It's not a good idea to owe money to another person.

IN

It's not a good idea to .... to another person.

3 I can't buy you everything you want because I just don't have enough money to do that!

MADE

I'm not .... so I can't buy you everything you want.

4 I think that young people live better lives than their grandparents, financially.

STANDARD

I think that young people have .... than their grandparents.

5 He's so rich – I can't imagine how much money he earns every week.

FORTUNE

He must be .... because he earns so much money every week.

6 I haven't got much money at the moment, so I can't buy that new mobile phone yet.

TIGHT

Money .... at the moment, so I can't buy that new mobile phone yet.

Listening
Sentence completion (Part 2)
▶ CB page 27

About the exam:
In the Listening paper, Part 2, you complete sentences using a word or a short phrase. You must write the exact word or words you hear, and the sentences come in the same order as in the recording.

Strategy:
- Read the instructions carefully and make sure you understand the context and who is speaking.
- Read the sentences and try to guess what kind of information you need to write, e.g. a job, a time or a month, and think about what part of speech it is.
- Listen and complete the sentences. If you miss an answer the first time, go on to the next sentence. You can complete any missed sentences when you listen for the second time.
- Check that your answers are grammatically correct and that you have not made any spelling mistakes.

1 ▶ 05 **You will hear a young naturalist called Steve Barnes talking to a group of students about his work and why it matters so much to him. For questions 1–10, listen and complete the sentences using a word or a short phrase.**

Steve first became interested in animals because he lived on a **(1)** .... as a child.

Steve particularly enjoyed getting the **(2)** .... after school.

Steve likes going **(3)** .... and rock-climbing in his spare time.

Steve uses the word **(4)** .... to describe the job he does.

According to Steve, **(5)** .... is the most important message of the TV programmes he makes.

Steve wants children to have a feeling of **(6)** .... with his programmes.

Steve gives the example of a time he was injured by falling over a **(7)** .... to show how spontaneous his programmes are.

Steve is pleased that his programmes have made children realise how changes in **(8)** .... affect the natural world.

According to Steve, some experts say that **(9)** .... has the most negative effect on children's connection with the natural world.

Steve feels thrilled to have discovered the biggest species of **(10)** .... on one of his expeditions.

Grammar
using modifiers for comparison
▶ CB page 28

1 **Complete quiz questions 1–6 with the comparative or superlative form of the adjectives in brackets.**

1 Which country has .... tourist industry? (*big*)

2 Where do you get .... weather all year round? (*sunny*)

3 Which city is .... – Melbourne or London? (*polluted*)

4 Which is .... mineral in the world? (*rare*)

5 Which country has .... students at maths? (*intelligent*)

6 Which country has .... record on environmental protection? (*good*)

2 **The answers (A–F) to the questions in Activity 1 contain mistakes with comparative and superlative forms. Correct the mistakes and match the answers with the questions.**

A Fewest than two or three crystals of painite, which is said to be the rarest, are found each year.

B Switzerland. But my country, Australia, is much worser than I thought.

C Yuma in Arizona. The sun shines for more that 90 percent of the time.

D In Korea students get by far the high scores in maths tests but they're not as better at some other subjects.

E France has the more tourist visitors, but China is getting more and more popular.

F London, though they are trying to get lesser people to drive their cars in the centre of the city.

3 **Choose the correct options in italics to complete the dialogue.**

A: What do you like **(1)** *more/most* about the place you come from?

B: Well, there are some amazing buildings, but that's not nearly **(2)** *as important as/more important than* the people. They're great.

A: Would you like to move back to your home town when you finish studying or are you **(3)** *happier/happiest* here?

B: I'm **(4)** *just as happy/far happier* living here than I would be back home. This is **(5)** *the best/the better* place to live in the world, in my opinion.

Speaking
Long turn (Part 2) ▶ CB page 29

1 ▶ 06 **Listen to the examiner giving a student some instructions and the student's response. Does she do what the examiner asks her to do?**

2 **Underline the correct alternatives to complete the extract from a speaking test. Then listen again and check your answers.**

These photographs are similar because they both show groups of people but they are **(1)** *very different/more different* in other ways. The first photograph shows people on a beach, **(2)** *and/whereas* the people in the second photograph are probably in a city or town as they are in some kind of sports stadium. In the first photograph, the people look **(3)** *as/like* they care about the environment because they are cleaning the beach, and they are working hard **(4)** *although/like* on the other hand the people in the second photograph look **(5)** *more relaxed/most relaxed* because it seems as though the football team has won a trophy. They all **(6)** *look/look like* happy. The people on the beach **(7)** *look as if/look* they are upset about the condition of the beach, **(8)** *although/even* they must be pleased to be doing something about it, and there are also children helping.

Reading
Multiple choice (Part 5)
▶ CB page 30

1 **You are going to read an article about singing and what it means to people. Read the article quickly and decide if the following statement is true or false.**

All the people involved with Rock Choir are non-professionals.

2 **Read the article again. For questions 1–6, choose the answer (A, B, C or D) which you think fits best according to the text.**

1 How does Wendy feel about signing up to Rock Choir?

  A She is completely convinced that this was the right decision.

  B She wishes she had done it sooner.

  C She hasn't enjoyed it as much as she thought she would.

  D She has found the pressure to learn to sing difficult.

2 What has Rock Choir meant for Wendy?

  A She has learnt to appreciate how talented people are.

  B She has been able to learn to read music.

  C She has thoroughly enjoyed being part of a group.

  D She has found a way to solve her own problems.

3 Why did Caroline Redman Lusher originally found Rock Choir?

  A She wanted to become a performing artist.

  B She was tired of teaching people who were not very talented.

  C She realised that singing helped people improve and feel better.

  D She wanted to get away from her home town.

4 What does 'they' in line 34 refer to?

  A tales

  B members

  C years

  D teachers

5 How are decisions made about what the Rock Choirs should sing?

  A The better choirs can choose but the others have to do what Caroline says.

  B The choir leaders decide which songs they like best.

  C All the choirs sing the same songs chosen by Caroline.

  D The choirs sing songs which Caroline prepares specially.

6 How does Caroline Redman Lusher account for the positive impact of Rock Choir?

  A She points out that they raise a lot of money for people in need.

  B She is reluctant to attribute the positive effects to one factor.

  C She emphasises that they are willing to perform almost anywhere.

  D She attributes it to the way members relate to one another.

3 **Match the underlined words in the text to the definitions.**

1 happening at that time

2 increased quickly to a high level

3 very careful and thorough

4 first in a planned series

5 improve your skill at doing something

6 learn something by repeating it many times

7 good or bad feelings that a particular person, place or situation seems to produce

8 understand something very clearly

9 try to help when someone is in a difficult situation

10 set of ideas or attitudes that are typical of a group

Why not join a Rock Choir?

Wendy Neale has had Thursdays circled in her diary every week for the past 11 years. It's when she attends her regular practice for Rock Choir, the hugely successful contemporary singing phenomenon. Already more than 24,000 people have joined some 320 choirs to learn to sing pop songs and classic tunes together.

'I've never had a moment of regret about joining, as it has given me untold fun ever since I started,' says Wendy, who signed up with the first ever Rock Choir set up in 2005. She has been a loyal member ever since. In that time she has learnt to sing everything from Beatles ballads to uplifting gospel songs and a huge variety in between. Whether it's a golden oldie or Beyoncé's latest download sensation, Wendy and the other choirs nationwide will <u>hone</u> it in the halls and hotel rooms they rehearse in. After weeks of <u>painstaking</u> practice, they get the chance to perform in venues ranging from shopping centres to Wembley Arena.

More of these choirs are due to spring up soon and many existing members share the same enthusiasm for Rock Choir as Wendy. 'I had no history or experience in choirs before I joined,' Wendy says. 'And not having to be able to read music or needing to audition really appealed to me. The <u>ethos</u> of Rock Choir is to be totally inclusive and not judge people on ability or talent. It's like one big family where everyone's welcome. I've made lots of good friends from the choir. Not only is everyone supportive when we are singing, but outside choir too. If anyone is having a bad time, the way the others <u>rally round</u> is incredible.'

Rock Choir was founded by professional singer and musician Caroline Redman Lusher, who first got the idea while teaching performing arts students who couldn't read music. So instead she taught them to sing by <u>rote</u> around the piano and their grades and confidence <u>soared</u>. Caroline decided to try the simple concept on others. She put out flyers where she lived asking if locals wanted to sing in a modern choir. After 70 people showed up at the <u>inaugural</u> coffee shop gathering, Caroline knew she was on to something.

Within six months plans were <u>underway</u> to start up Rock Choirs across the country. Each had a trained musician as its leader who would follow the model established by Caroline. There are now 66 leaders and more being recruited to satisfy growing demand. 'I felt I'd come across something that did lots of good and made people really happy, too,' says Caroline. 'I strongly feel now it's my responsibility to carry that on. We often hear amazing tales from our members who tell us that they haven't sung for 20 or 30 or more years after teachers at school said they were useless at singing. And now their confidence is there, they're performing at some of the country's best-known venues, when before they didn't think they could sing a note.' line 34

The choirs are open to all aged 18 and above. Both sexes are welcome, although by far the majority of members are female. After being welcomed, new members can progress at their own pace. The songs are chosen by Caroline who works out how the choir leaders can best teach them. More experienced choirs might work on trickier arrangements while newer ones start on more simple pieces.

Rock Choir members often carry out flash mob appearances at both big and small locations, and also appear at charity events to support and fundraise for good causes. 'It's hard to <u>pin down</u> whether it's the singing, the friendship, the fulfilment from doing a new activity or the positive <u>vibes</u> our members feel that they most like. It's probably a combination of everything,' says Caroline. 'I'm still amazed that something so natural as singing can transform lives in such a simple way.'

Vocabulary

-ed adjectives and prepositions
▶ CB page 31

1 **Find and correct the mistakes in sentences 1–6 below.**

1 I get really annoyed of people talking loudly on their mobile phones during concerts.

2 I'm quite frightened with snakes, though I know it's stupid!

3 I'm really worried with the environment; we really have to do more to look after the planet.

4 My brother is really interested on sport – he loves it.

5 I get quite embarrassed of bad behaviour in sports events; I feel really bad about it.

6 We're going on holiday next week and I'm so excited with it!

2 **Complete sentences 1–6 with the correct form of the words in the box.**

| annoy | embarrass | excite | frustrate |
| interest | worry | | |

1 I often go red and feel incredibly .... when people praise me.

2 It's quite .... when people talk loudly on their mobiles in quiet places.

3 I get very .... about holidays.

4 I was very .... about my sister recently when she had a wisdom tooth removed.

5 I find history very .... , particularly the sixteenth century.

6 I get very .... when people stop me doing what I want to do.

Grammar

present perfect and past simple
▶ CB page 32

1 **Choose the correct options in italics to complete the text.**

I **(1)** *have been/was* interested in photography all my life. I **(2)**'*ve owned/owned* about ten different cameras over the years. I **(3)** *started/'ve started* with quite a cheap camera that my parents **(4)** *bought/have bought* me for my fifteenth birthday. I **(5)** *used to get/have got* the films developed at a local photography shop. Of course, I **(6)** *haven't had to/didn't have to* do that for a long time now. Digital photography **(7)** *has been/was* really bad for shops like that. Many of them **(8)** *have gone/went* out of business.

2 **Complete the text with the present perfect or present perfect continuous form of the verbs in brackets.**

HORSE MAD

Every Christmas and every birthday throughout my childhood I always put one thing and one thing only on the list of things I wanted: a horse. I **(0)** *have been* (be) mad about horses for almost as long as I can remember but it's only recently that I **(1)** .... (*actually start*) learning to ride. Apparently, riding **(2)** .... (*become*) popular with a lot of adults so I'm not alone. I **(3)** .... (*have*) lessons at a local riding school for about two months now. I go twice a week so I **(4)** .... (*have*) about fifteen lessons so far. I'm really impressed with the instructor and with my horse, Daisy. I **(5)** .... (*learn*) so much from her. She's incredibly kind and patient with me though she **(6)** .... (*get*) a little bit cross a couple of times. I **(7)** .... (*read*) about the benefits of riding lately as well. Apart from all the physical benefits, riding improves self-confidence, helps you learn to face risks and makes you much more self-disciplined. Riding is more than just a hobby for me too. It **(8)** .... (*give*) my life meaning.

Use of English

Open cloze (Part 2)
▶ CB page 33

About the exam:

In the Reading and Use of English paper, Part 2, you read a text with eight gaps. The missing words may be grammatical, e.g. parts of verbs, determiners (*this*, *those*, etc.), connectors (*however*, *moreover*, etc.), *as* and *like*, or vocabulary, e.g. phrasal verbs or collocations such as *do your homework*.

Strategy:

• Read the title and the whole text to make sure you understand it.
• Look at the words on both sides of each gap.
• Decide what kind of word is missing.

1 **Complete sentences 1–6 with a grammatical word, collocation or phrasal verb.**

1 Some people find music can cheer them .... when they feel low.

2 Make .... you study hard before an exam.

3 I'm so busy that I don't know how I'm going to get .... the amount of homework I have to do.

4 It's easy to .... in touch with old friends from school on the internet.

5 I prefer doing sports .... tennis to sitting reading.

6 I've always thought of you .... my best friend.

2 For questions 1–8, read the text below and think of the word which best fits each gap. Use only one word in each gap. There is an example at the beginning (0).

Is that glass really half empty or half full?

What is really important in life? Sometimes it's good to sit back and think **(0)** _about_ where you are right now and what you hope to be good **(1)** .... in the future. Having aims and objectives is crucial, **(2)** .... you must also appreciate what you have already and should be thankful for. Everybody has ups and downs, good days and bad days. Sometimes something **(3)** .... may seem to be a huge problem one day can seem very insignificant the next. It's vital to **(4)** .... things in perspective. Always believe that **(5)** .... bad you may feel about something, there's always somebody out there who **(6)** .... had a tougher or more difficult day than you. If you can't appreciate this fact, you're likely to feel more unhappy than you need to. Of **(7)** .... , that doesn't mean you can always be cheerful and smiling, but there are a lot of good things out there, so cheer **(8)** .... People who say a half-full glass of water is half empty are considered to be pessimists – so try to see that glass of water as being half full! You'll feel much happier!

Writing
Article (Part 2)
▶ CB page 34

About the exam:
In Part 2 of the Writing paper, you choose to write one task from three options. One of these may be an article. The purpose of an article is to interest and engage the reader.

Strategy:
• Read the task carefully to identify what you must include.
• Think of ways of interesting the reader, e.g. colourful language, rhetorical questions.
• Think of an interesting introduction and conclusion.

1 Read the task and then match the ideas that some students have had for their articles (1–7) with the reasons they gave (A–G).

You see this advertisement on an English language website.

Articles wanted
An activity I would never give up!
What is the best activity you do? Why is it important to you? Why wouldn't you want to give it up?
Write us an article answering these questions.
We will put the best article on our website.

Write your **article**. Write **140–190** words.

Activities
1 I know it sounds strange but I think I will go on studying throughout my life.
2 I would never give up visiting my grandparents.
3 I've been practising meditation for about three years now and I could never do without it.
4 I would never give up playing tennis at our local club.
5 I just couldn't live without playing the guitar.
6 No matter how old I get, I will never stop surfing.
7 Working as a volunteer is more important to me than anything else I do.

Reasons
A The exhilaration you feel on your board is just incredible.
B There's always something new to learn.
C It has really improved my concentration.
D I make new friends, meet old ones and it certainly keeps me fit.
E I love being able to make music for my friends.
F I know I'm using my time to make a difference and that's what matters.
G It really means a lot to them to see my cousins and me every weekend.

2 Look at the titles and opening paragraphs below. Which one is better?

A Something I would never give up: riding my quad bike

I do a lot of different activities but the one I like most is riding my quad bike. I've only had the bike for a couple of months but I enjoy riding it so much, I don't think I will ever give it up. It is very important to me.

B Life just wouldn't be the same

I enjoy a lot of the things I do but if you asked me if there was one activity I liked more than the others, my answer would have to be singing in a rock band. I honestly don't think I could ever willingly give it up. Let me tell you why.

3 Look at the conclusions to two more articles. Which one is better?

A That is why I would never give up such an important activity. You should try it too. It's very good for you.
B So, whatever people say, however old I get, whatever happens to me, I don't think I would ever give up doing martial arts. It's what keeps my body and soul together.

4 Write your article using the task information in Activity 1.

Reading
Multiple matching (Part 7)
▶ CB page 38

1 You are going to read a newspaper article about a man who swam in the Arctic Ocean. Read the article quickly. Which of the following are not mentioned?

boats   clothes   ice   polar bears   scientists

2 Read the article again more carefully. For questions 1–10, choose from the sections (A–D). The sections may be chosen more than once.

Which paragraph:

says that an expert considers Mr Pugh different to other people?	**1**
suggests that Mr Pugh had great admiration for someone?	**2**
shows that Mr Pugh had mixed feelings about his swim?	**3**
suggests that Mr Pugh quickly recovered from his swim?	**4**
describes three things that would cause death for other people if they undertook a similar swim?	**5**
says that Mr Pugh has to persuade himself to do a swim like this?	**6**
states that researchers find it difficult to understand how Mr Pugh can swim in cold water?	**7**
explains what encouraged Mr Pugh to reach the end of such a difficult swim?	**8**
mentions the way Mr Pugh learnt that he had his special ability?	**9**
states that Mr Pugh is unique for another reason?	**10**

3 Find words in the article to match definitions 1–8 below.

1 glasses made of plastic or glass with a rubber edge used for protecting your eyes (paragraph A)
2 extremely happy and excited (paragraph A)
3 next to (paragraph B)
4 extremely painful (paragraph B)
5 moves (paragraph C)
6 natural ability (paragraph C)
7 carefully watching and checking to see how something changes over a period of time (paragraph D)
8 great physical pain (paragraph D)

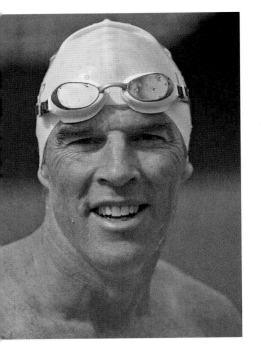

A very chilly swim

Auslan Cramb looks into a North Pole swimmer's unique body heat trick

A Dressed only in swimming trunks, a cap and goggles Lewis Gordon Pugh spent nearly 19 minutes yesterday in the coldest water ever endured by a man who lived to tell the tale. Mr Pugh, the only man to carry out endurance swims in all five oceans, swam 1km along a temporary crack in the ice of the Arctic Ocean in 18 minutes and 50 seconds. It should not in fact be possible to swim at the North Pole at all but an increase in global air temperatures has reduced the amount of sea ice. As a result, patches of open sea are appearing in summer. Scientists predict that by 2040 there may be no sea ice left. Mr Pugh, 37, said he hoped his effort would draw attention to the effects of global warming and would put pressure on world leaders to cut carbon emissions. He added: 'I am obviously ecstatic to have succeeded but this swim is a triumph and a tragedy: a triumph that I could swim in such ferocious conditions but a tragedy that it's possible to swim at the North Pole.'

B Mr Pugh, who is an international ambassador for the World Wildlife Foundation, spent months acclimatising his body to extreme cold. His ability to survive in such an extreme environment has baffled scientists for years, but he admitted yesterday that he considered giving up during his toughest challenge. He said he was spurred on by the presence of Jorgen Amundsen, a relative of Roald Amundsen, the first man to reach the South Pole. The Norwegian skied on the ice alongside Mr Pugh during the swim. 'The water was absolutely black,' said Mr Pugh. 'I was in excruciating pain from beginning to end and I nearly quit on a few occasions but I just kept on looking at Jorgen Amundsen. I couldn't give up in front of a relative of Roald Amundsen.'

C Most people would die quickly in a water temperature of -1.8 degrees Celsius (29 degrees Fahrenheit) through a rapid process of hyperventilation, shock and drowning. But Mr Pugh is different. His cold water endurance swims are made possible by a phenomenon he calls 'anticipatory thermogenesis', the ability to elevate his core body temperature while psyching himself up before he enters the water. 'As soon as I enter cold water my body shunts all my warm blood to my core to protect my vital organs. It then generates incredible heat,' he said. 'Before I even enter the water, I am able to elevate my core body temperature by as much as 1.4 degrees Celsius. This phenomenon has, to our knowledge, not been noted in any other human.' Mr Pugh discovered his unusual gift by accident when he began to perspire and feel thirsty while staring at freezing water before an earlier Arctic dip.

D Professor Tim Noakes, a sports scientist who has been monitoring the swimmer, said Pugh had pushed the boundaries of what was humanly possible. 'At the end of the swim Lewis was showing obvious signs of distress but he never faltered and his performance was his best yet. There has never been anyone like him. He was sweating before he left the ship and got into the water, and within one hour of finishing he was walking around in a T-shirt, shorts and flip flops. The rest of us are wearing multiple layers of clothing, including gloves and hats.' Professor Noakes said that while Mr Pugh was able to raise the temperature around his heart, lungs and brain before a swim, the temperature of his muscles dropped to 30 degrees Celsius during the event, which would prove fatal for most people.

Vocabulary
compound words
▶ CB page 39

1 Complete sentences 1-6 with the words in the box. There is one extra word you do not need to use.

breath-taking	drawbacks	everyday
extraordinary	far-fetched	side-effects
sub-zero		

1 She takes fascinating photographs of simple .... objects like spoons, paperclips and clothes pegs.

2 My grandmother had to stop taking the tablets because the .... were very unpleasant.

3 The plot of the book struck me as ridiculously ....

4 He has the .... ability to withstand extreme temperatures.

5 One of the .... of a skiing holiday is that you need expensive equipment and waterproof clothing.

6 Images of the .... views are shown alongside small maps indicating how to get there.

Grammar
definite, indefinite and zero articles
▶ CB page 40

1 Find and correct the mistakes with articles in sentences 1–10.

1 That's a lovely house over there and it's got the beautiful garden.

2 We had dinner last night in a most expensive restaurant in town.

3 How often do you play the golf?

4 I had to go to dentist last week as my tooth was very painful!

5 Where did you have the lunch yesterday?

6 The most important thing we can all do for planet is to recycle more.

7 I'm staying at the home today.

8 I love a snow – it's great for skiing!

9 I could hear a rain beating on the roof of the tent all night.

10 I could see it was raining, so I just grabbed the umbrella from the collection in the cupboard.

2 Complete the newspaper article with *a/an*, *the* or *(–)* for no article.

Report from Antarctica

In March, I'm joining **(0)** ___–___ other scientists in Punta Arenas, **(1)** ___ southernmost town in **(2)** ___ Chile. We're departing on **(3)** ___ special research vessel heading for **(4)** ___ South Shetland Islands situated off **(5)** ___ Antarctic Peninsula for a thirty-two-day trip, and while we're at **(6)** ___ sea, we'll be collecting environmental data from **(7)** ___ waters surrounding **(8)** ___ islands. We're looking for any long-term trends and changes in **(9)** ___ Antarctic ecosystem. Antarctica is famous for having **(10)** ___ most treacherous seas on **(11)** ___ Earth, and during **(12)** ___ last trip we got hammered with **(13)** ___ bad weather. Not only does this make **(14)** ___ life on board pretty uncomfortable, but it also causes all sorts of sampling problems. **(15)** ___ last month, **(16)** ___ scientific team lost valuable and expensive gear. Of course, all this is normal when you're working in **(17)** ___ Antarctica and it's what makes **(18)** ___ Southern Ocean such an exciting environment to work in. Every year is **(19)** ___ new adventure and one I look forward to – even though **(20)** ___ dangers there are very real!

Use of English
Word formation (Part 3)
▶ CB page 41

1 Use the prefixes in box A to make the opposites of the adjectives and verbs in box B. You can use the prefixes more than once.

A   dis-   im-   ir-   mis-   un-

B   ~~advantage~~   loyal   fortunate   healthy   mature
patient   responsible   successful   understand

0 _disadvantage_	**3** ___	**6** ___
1 ___	**4** ___	**7** ___
2 ___	**5** ___	**8** ___

2 Complete sentences 1–4 with the correct form of the words in brackets. Add a negative prefix where necessary.

1 The first expeditions to ascend Everest were ___ and several climbers died. (*success*)

2 I feel quite ___ if I criticise my friend about anything. (*loyal*)

3 He's always having accidents. He's very ___ . (*fortunate*)

4 Wait a minute! Don't be so ___ ! (*patient*)

3 For questions 1–8, read the text below. Use the word given in capitals at the end of some of the lines to form a word that fits in the gap in the same line.

Driven to extremes

People used to go on holiday for **(0)** _relaxation_ .   **RELAX**
Nowadays, however, there seems to be a real obsession with holidaying in a very different way – taking on extreme challenges. What began as a small number of people climbing Everest or crossing the Antarctic has developed into a **(1)** ___ industry. For   **SUCCESS**
those who choose to undertake **(2)** ___ events such   **COMPETE**
as a race across Death Valley, the enterprise can be dangerous and the chances of **(3)** ___ for those who   **SURVIVE**
are **(4)** ___ in such conditions depends on experts   **EXPERIENCE**
making sure they do not set off **(5)** ___ . Many do it   **PREPARE**
because they find their everyday lives **(6)** ___ and so   **SATISFY**
they dream of adventure. Instead of spending their time off in **(7)** ___ cafés enjoying glorious sunshine,   **PLEASE**
people are suffering, attempting more and more outrageous things. Some people do it to raise money for charity but others want exciting and dangerous experiences, so they look for new and possibly **(8)** ___ challenges to face.   **RESPONSIBLE**

Listening
Multiple choice (Part 4)
▶ CB page 42

1 ▶ 07 **You will hear an interview with Alan Preston, a young man who sailed round the world alone at the age of sixteen. For questions 1–7, choose the best answer (A, B or C).**

1 How does Alan describe himself as a child?

  A keen to follow in his father's footsteps

  B interested in dangerous activities

  C willing to try anything new

2 Why does Alan say he started sailing seriously?

  A He wanted to please his parents.

  B He hoped to repeat a good experience.

  C He intended to follow his own ambitions.

3 How did Alan feel about preparing to sail round the world?

  A It was difficult getting financial help.

  B It was hard getting his whole family to agree.

  C It was tough dealing with personal criticism.

4 When he started the trip, Alan

  A found it too physically demanding.

  B was upset by difficulties with the boat.

  C worried about the prospect of loneliness.

5 Alan said that the worst moment of his trip

  A gave him confidence to cope with anything.

  B meant he had to use special equipment for the first time.

  C was challenging because of unexpected weather conditions.

6 Alan explains that he continues to sail because of

  A the emotion he gets from being at sea.

  B the competitive nature of the sport.

  C the things he sees while sailing.

7 What is Alan's most important advice for other young sailors?

  A Keep sailing in perspective.

  B Get the best advice you can.

  C Prepare differently for each trip.

Vocabulary
idioms: the body
▶ CB page 43

1 **Match 1–8 with A–H to make idioms connected with the body. Use two of the verbs twice.**

1	get	**A**	a straight face about something
2	catch	**B**	cold feet about something
3	keep	**C**	your head around something
4	put	**D**	your foot down about something
5	come	**E**	eye to eye with someone about something
6	see	**F**	someone's eye
		G	face to face with something
		H	an eye on something

2 **Replace the underlined words in sentences 1–8 with an idiom using the part(s) of the body given in brackets.**

Example: *I don't enjoy working with Josh – we never seem to be able to agree about anything. (eye)*

I don't enjoy working with Josh – we never seem to see eye to eye about anything.

1 That new car must have been incredibly expensive! (*arm, leg*)

2 I couldn't stop myself laughing when he wore those ridiculous clothes to the party. (*face*)

3 I'm getting pretty nervous about the meeting next week. (*feet*)

4 I feel really ill so I don't feel like going shopping this morning. (*face*)

5 I'm finding it hard to understand the new sickness policy at work. (*head*)

6 I'm sorry but I must pay attention to the time because I can't miss the bus. (*eye*)

7 I'm always scared of saying the wrong thing at work. (*foot*)

8 When I was shopping, that new camera really attracted my attention – I think I'll buy it next week. (*eye*)

Grammar
narrative forms
▶ CB page 44

1 **Find and correct the mistakes with narrative forms in sentences 1–10. There are mistakes in six of the sentences. Tick the sentences that are correct.**

1 I walked down the street when I saw my friend Brenda getting out of a sports car.

2 The man who was driving it was looking slightly familiar.

3 I was sure I had seen him somewhere before.

4 As he drove off, I was realising that I had met him at a party at Brenda's boyfriend's house.

5 He had been talking to my boyfriend just before we left the party.

6 Later that night, my boyfriend had told me that the man had been telling him a story about a friend who had disappeared.

7 Apparently this person had been missing for several months before he was found living in France.

8 He had been working as a waiter in a restaurant and using a false name.

9 The man who told my boyfriend the story had had dinner in the restaurant when he recognised the missing man.

10 I still wonder what Brenda did getting out of his car that day.

2 **Complete the story with the correct past form of the verbs in brackets.**

A would-be lifeguard

I **(1)** .... (jog) along the beach with my boyfriend when I **(2)** .... (notice) a man on a surfboard quite a long way out who **(3)** .... (wave) his arms around frantically. I **(4)** .... (not stop) to think and **(5)** .... (run) into the water to try and save him. Only a month before I **(6)** .... (complete) a special training programme for lifeguards and I **(7)** .... (want) to try out what I **(8)** .... (learn).

I **(9)** .... (swim) as fast as I could to where I **(10)** .... (see) the man on the surfboard but when I **(11)** .... (get) there he **(12)** .... (disappear) completely. I **(13)** .... (look) around desperately but he **(14)** .... (be) nowhere to be seen.

I **(15)** .... (feel) really terrible. It **(16)** .... (be) my first opportunity to rescue someone and I **(17)** .... (fail) dismally. I **(18)** .... (walk) sadly along the beach looking for my boyfriend when I **(19)** .... (see) the man. He **(20)** .... (talk) to my boyfriend and they **(21)** .... (laugh)! It **(22)** .... (turn out) that they **(23)** .... (know) each other at university but **(24)** .... (lose) contact. The man **(25)** .... (wave) to attract my boyfriend's attention, not because he **(26)** .... (drown).

Speaking
Collaborative task (Part 3)
▶ CB page 45

About the exam:
In the Speaking test, Part 3, you are given a question to discuss for two minutes. There are some prompts with ideas to help you, and the examiner listens to what you say. The examiner then asks you to make a decision.

Strategy:
• You don't have to talk about all the ideas on the task sheet. Say as much as you can about each one before you move on to the next.

1 ▶ 08 **Two students are discussing the task below. Listen and complete their conversation.**

> Some people say that it's a good idea for young people to take on physical challenges, and other people disagree.

learning to cope with difficulties

taking risks — **Is it a good idea for young people to take on physical challenges?** — having fun

getting new experiences   gaining self-confidence

A: OK. Let's talk about taking risks. **(1)** ...., no one should put themselves in danger.

B: **(2)** .... – I think that young people can become much more confident if they manage to do difficult things, especially on their own.

A: **(3)** ...., but not everyone is brave like that, and it may actually have the opposite effect and make them less confident.

B: **(4)** ...., but it's always a good idea for young people to get new experiences.

A: **(5)** .... – and it's difficult for anyone to do that if they never take any risks at all.

B: Plus, **(6)** .... it can be fun! You don't know about that unless you try.

2 **Now decide which is the best reason for young people to take on physical challenges.**

Writing
Essay (Part 1)
▶ CB page 46

1 **Read the task below. What ideas could you write about for point 3?**

In your English class you have been talking about the environment. Now, your teacher has asked you to write an essay.

Write an essay using all the notes and give reasons for your point of view.

What can we do as individuals to help the environment?
Notes
Write about:
1 recycling
2 transport
3 .... (your own idea)

2 **These sentences were written to answer the task in Activity 1. Complete the sentences with the best word or phrase from the box. There may be more than one possibility.**

apart from   as a result   as well as
because of this   in addition to   in my view
in order to   I believe   would lead to

1 .... , it is important for every individual to take responsibility for the environment.

2 People should use the same shopping bag over and over again, ... cut down on plastic.

3 It is easy to recycle paper, and this .... fewer trees being cut down.

4 If we cycled everywhere, there would be fewer cars on the road and .... there would be a decrease in fumes.

5 .... cycling, people should also walk more; .... saving energy the consequence would be that people would be healthier.

6 People should turn lights off when they leave a room; this would save energy .... money.

7 .... that if people didn't leave their computers on standby, they would save energy.

8 People use too much energy, and .... the ozone layer is getting thinner.

3 **Which idea in the sentences in Activity 2 was not included in the task and was the student's own idea?**

a recycling   b transport   c saving energy

4 **Read this student's essay answering the task in Activity 1 and choose the correct linking words in italics.**

Many people feel that it is not worth doing anything on their own to help the environment, since one individual cannot make a difference. **(1)** *However/In addition*, there are some things that **(2)** *unless/if* we all do them, then we can improve the situation with the ozone layer.

The first thing we can do is recycle our waste products. People should **(3)** *also/too* use the same shopping bag over and over again, **(4)** *in order to/such as* cut down on plastic.

Another idea is choosing the transport we use. **(5)** *As well as/Instead of* driving cars, if we all cycled everywhere, this would mean that there were fewer cars on the road and **(6)** *as a result/following* there would be a decrease in fumes. This would also make people healthier.

I believe that saving energy is something that everyone can do, **(7)** *and/while* if people didn't leave their computers on standby, they would not use so much electricity and would save energy.

(8) *While/What's more* I agree that all of these things don't make a difference if only one person does them; if we all do them, then we can start to look after our environment.

5 **Now write your own answer to the task below. Try to use linking words from Activities 2 and 4.**

In your English class you have been talking about the natural world. Now, your teacher has asked you to write an essay.

Write an essay using all the notes and give reasons for your point of view.

Is it important to have parks and green spaces in cities? Give your opinion.
Notes
Write about:
1 wildlife
2 beauty
3 .... (your own idea)

6 **Check the length of your answer. It should be 140–190 words.**

Multiple-choice cloze (Part 1)

For questions 1–8, read the text below and decide which answer (A, B, C or D) best fits each gap. There is an example at the beginning (0).

The science of happiness

Some scientists believe that asking people how happy they are is **(0)** _A, similar to_ asking them about an event they've attended in the past – there's a lot they **(1)** .... no notice of during the experience, so how do they know? These scientists think that anyone studying happiness should pay more **(2)** .... to people's experiences at the time they occur, not afterwards.

Other scientists say that we are actually **(3)** .... up of our memories. They suggest that studying moment-to-moment experiences at the time **(4)** .... too much emphasis on temporary pleasures, and that happiness goes **(5)** .... than that. They identify three key **(6)** .... for happiness: pleasure, engagement (how involved we are with family, work, romance and hobbies) and meaning (how we use our personal strengths to achieve important **(7)** ....). It is interesting that, **(8)** .... to what might be expected, pleasure seems to play the smallest part in what makes us happy.

0	**A** similar to	**B** close to	**C** typical of	**D** consists of
1	**A** gave	**B** took	**C** got	**D** kept
2	**A** focus	**B** concentration	**C** attention	**D** regard
3	**A** made	**B** built	**C** created	**D** developed
4	**A** sets	**B** puts	**C** fixes	**D** rests
5	**A** stronger	**B** lower	**C** deeper	**D** greater
6	**A** ingredients	**B** parts	**C** factors	**D** items
7	**A** intentions	**B** plans	**C** marks	**D** goals
8	**A** against	**B** opposing	**C** contrary	**D** contrast

Open cloze (Part 2)

For questions 9–16, read the text below and think of the word which best fits each gap. Use only one word in each gap. There is an example at the beginning (0).

More than just a pretty face?

There are many stories of dolphins helping people in trouble, **(0)** _like_ like saving swimmers from shark attacks by gathering round them or shepherding them to safety. **(9)** .... these stories are true, why do dolphins do it and **(10)** .... makes them behave in this way? Scientists **(11)** .... have studied them are not entirely sure. For dolphins to act together as a group to save humans implies that **(12)** .... is some sort of code of ethics among dolphins, but there is little evidence for that. The **(13)** .... likely explanation is that they instinctively respond to the appearance of predators like sharks by herding weaker members of their own group into **(14)** .... safe place – and there is proof that dolphins do cooperate with **(15)** .... other to ward off danger. Maybe they just mistake swimmers for part of their group, which would mean that dolphins don't have genuine feelings of kindness towards humans. **(16)** .... may be that their smiling appearance simply gives people the wrong idea.

Word formation (Part 3)

For questions 17–24, read the text below. Use the word given in capitals at the end of some of the lines to form a word that fits in the gap in the same line. There is an example at the beginning (0).

Why do they do it?

People are attracted to attempting extreme activities for a **(0)** _variety_ of reasons. Some enjoy the challenge, others the feeling of **(17)** .... they get from testing themselves. So although their actual **(18)** .... may differ, people who participate in extreme sports probably share an inability to accept all the **(19)** .... that most of us think of as normal. They experience a sense of **(20)** .... with the routine of everyday life, and feel a need to push the boundaries of what is possible, to see how far they can go. Is this similar to simply being **(21)** .... ? Possibly, but it may be more to do with having a dream.

VARY

EXCITE

MOTIVATE

LIMIT

SATISFY

COMPETE

Of course **(22)** .... athletes who train for extreme events like the triathlon or the marathon may hope for **(23)** .... rewards, but primarily it seems they like being different. They enjoy the feeling of being set apart from other people by their **(24)** .... , which are things most of us would fear to do.

PROFESSION

FINANCE

ACHIEVE

Key word transformation (Part 4)

For questions 25–30, complete the second sentence so that it has a similar meaning to the first sentence, using the word given. Do not change the word given. You must use between two and five words, including the word given. Here is an example (0).

Example:

0 Please don't drive so fast – this is a dangerous road.

MORE

Please _drive more slowly_ .... – this is a dangerous road.

25 Nothing irritates me more than getting hundreds of spam emails.

MORE

There is nothing .... getting hundreds of spam emails.

26 The tennis game was so exciting that the spectators cheered loudly at the end.

WERE

The spectators .... the tennis game that they cheered loudly at the end.

27 I'm very interested in learning about the culture of other countries.

IS

Learning about the culture of other countries .... me.

28 I find it very worrying if things go wrong on holiday.

GET

I .... things going wrong on holiday.

29 I get bored by people who talk too much.

FIND

I .... when people talk too much.

30 I had never seen a glacier before I went to Norway.

I

When I was in Norway .... the first time.

5 Eat your heart out

Vocabulary
food
▶ CB page 48

1 Complete sentences 1–5 with the words in the box.

high-fat	low-salt	vegetarian	vitamins	well-balanced

1 I never eat meat – I follow a strict _____ diet.
2 People who are overweight are rarely told to follow a _____ diet.
3 It's good to give children a _____ diet, including meat, fruit and sugar.
4 I love fruit, vegetables and so on; I know I'm getting a diet rich in _____ .
5 Older people may be advised to follow a _____ diet for health reasons.

Grammar
expressions of quantity
▶ CB page 49

1 Choose the correct words in italics to complete the sentences.

1 Would you like *some/a few* rice with your chicken?
2 I mustn't eat too *many/much* chocolate – it's bad for me!
3 People who eat too *much/many* salt can suffer from high blood pressure.
4 I drink *hardly any/a few* coffee; if I drink too *many/much*, I can't sleep.
5 I buy very *few/little* eggs as I keep chickens, so I have new-laid eggs.
6 I eat *hardly any/a few* meat – I prefer vegetables!
7 There is always *many/a lot of* news about food scares these days.
8 There are *lots of/much* fantastic desserts at that new restaurant!

2 Complete sentences 1–8 with *few, a few, little* or *a little.*

1 I knew very _____ people at the party, so I didn't stay long.
2 _____ of us are going to have a barbecue in the garden tonight. Do you fancy coming?
3 Please could I have _____ sugar – this coffee is rather strong.
4 I've got _____ free time this week so I can do the work if you like.
5 I've eaten so many already that there are only _____ chocolates left!
6 I knew very _____ about Thai food so I bought a cookery book to learn more.
7 I know _____ people who enjoy very spicy food, but not many.
8 People say that _____ knowledge goes a long way!

subject/verb agreement
▶ CB page 49

3 **Choose the correct options in italics to complete the sentences.**

1 Eating too much sugar *is/are* bad for young children.
2 Most of my friends *eats/eat* fast food regularly.
3 Not many people *enjoy/enjoys* raw vegetables.
4 There *was/were* few people in the restaurant.
5 It's good that there *is/are* lots of advice about healthy lifestyles.

Use of English
Open cloze (Part 2)
▶ CB page 50

1 **Read the text below and think of the word which best fits each gap. Use only one word in each gap. There is an example at the beginning (0).**

Food, glorious food

These days it's very hard to get people to agree **(0)** on anything. But there's one thing we can all accept – people like food! However, what makes good food is **(1)** .... a universal concept – something considered repulsive in one part of the world is a delicious lunch in another. For example, many of us **(2)** .... been brought up to believe that insects are for swatting rather **(3)** .... eating, but in fact **(4)** .... are an important part of the diet in many places and provide a valuable source of protein. Perhaps the problem really is that we have become too unadventurous – we are now so **(5)** .... to vacuum-packed, tasteless ready-made meals that we are unwilling **(6)** .... try anything unusual. Yet many less obvious combinations of food can change our tastes – simple touches **(7)** .... combining carrots with sugar enhances their flavour – and how about trying strawberries with a bit **(8)** .... pepper? There's food out there for everyone and if you look hard enough, you are sure to find something you love.

2 **Check the answers in Activity 1 and find an example of**

1 a comparative.
2 a verb + preposition.
3 a quantifier.
4 a pronoun.
5 an auxiliary.

Listening
Sentence completion (Part 2)
▶ CB page 51

1 **Look at the text below and match the type of missing information (A–D) to sentences 1–5.**

A adjective
B number
C noun (x2)
D noun – name of a subject

2 ▶ 09 **You will hear a woman called Terri Preston talking about her unusual job. For questions 1–10, complete the sentences.**

The horse nutritionist

Terri studied **(1)** .... as her main subject at university.

Terri takes part in **(2)** .... to monitor the health of horses.

Terri was surprised to find that horses eat **(3)** .... kilos of grass every day.

One day Terri monitored very **(4)** .... horses which she found physically difficult.

Terri does not like doing **(5)** .... any more than she enjoys meetings.

Terri uses the word **(6)** .... to describe how she feels about answering questions on the phone.

Terri is annoyed about the way **(7)** .... is provided for her work.

Terri says that the best approach for people to take to a diet is **(8)** .... rather than reducing what they eat.

Terri uses the example of **(9)** .... as something people should eat less of if they enjoy chocolate.

Terri criticises some people in her industry for not being **(10)** .... enough.

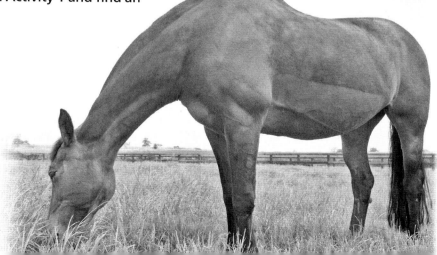

Reading
Multiple choice (Part 5)
▶ CB page 52

1 You are going to read an article about a woman who tried out a new kind of food. Read the text once quickly and choose the best title.

1   Is powdered food the future? Huel put to the test
2   It's nutritious and delicious: I'm going with Huel
3   Give me a hamburger every time: Huel is not for me

Last week, I posted a picture of my supper on Facebook. Never before has a post about a meal drawn so much <u>controversy</u> from friends. The reason? I was about to tuck into some Huel, a vegan powdered food that claims to contain everything the body needs, according to current government guidelines on <u>nutrition</u>.

This was on day 10 of my journey with Huel, the powdered food which has become something of a sensation. It sold out three times in the first month after its launch last year. Company founder Julian Hearn said his plan was not to <u>replace</u> food in our diets, but to offer a healthy, sustainable alternative to junk food and ready meals. After taking the stuff for three weeks it's a concept I've surprised myself by buying into – and I'm not alone. Some 400,000 Huel meals have been sold since June, in more than 30 countries.

Huel comes in a large, plain white bag with a scoop and instructions. One level scoop of Huel (38g) equates to 156 calories. You're advised to use an online calorie counter to calculate how many calories you should be consuming. At 167 cm and 63 kg and with a very active lifestyle, I need 2,233 calories daily to maintain my weight. I began my adventure with Huel one busy evening when, <u>engrossed</u> in work, I didn't want to stop to cook.

The instructions suggest adding some flavour when you start and to introduce Huel slowly. I blended three scoops with 550ml of water and a banana: a 'meal', according to the packet, and the equivalent of eating a sandwich. The first gulp of creamy, vanilla-tasting liquid seemed harmless, but the following sips got smaller as I <u>struggled</u> to swallow it and couldn't finish, mainly because I found it so filling. Not eating felt strange but I went to bed feeling satisfied and with no ill effects. Ordinarily, I eat very healthy meals, so I notice when I've consumed any kind of junk but not with Huel, despite feeling rather worried when I looked at the lists on the label. The main ingredients are oats, pea protein, brown rice protein and flaxseeds followed by what looked like a load of chemicals. According to Julian Hearn these provide vitamins and minerals.

Over the first few days, I hated the sugary smell of Huel and its sweet taste, but by the end of the week, I'd got the hang of it: one meal a day, best consumed for breakfast. I found it really useful during a busy working week. It was highly convenient having my dishwasher virtually unused and my rubbish bin empty. Besides, because I intentionally restricted my calorie intake to rid my body of some excess weight I'd put on over Christmas, by the end of the week I had lost 3 kilos.

Week two was harder. On two Huel meals a day I started to really miss eating. I love cooking and eating is a highly social occasion for me. But when I did sit down to a proper meal, I savoured every single mouthful. Huel had <u>heightened</u> my appreciation for food. Most encouragingly though, I was feeling great. There was no difference in energy levels at the gym and my body tolerated it well.

In week three, I managed two full days of only Huel before I broke. I missed mealtimes and the <u>therapy</u> of cooking after a long day. But even with the experiment over, I continued with one Huel meal a day – especially when on the run, which is exactly how the powder is meant to be used.

Ironically, if I'd posted a picture of a burger from a fast-food chain on my Facebook page, it would have attracted plenty of thumbs up – but it's junk. Huel, in my opinion, is not.

line 38

line 40

2 Read the text again. For questions 1–6, choose the answer (A, B, C or D) which you think fits best according to the text.

1 What does the author think about Julian Hearn's claims for his product?

  A She finds them surprising.

  B She accepts them reluctantly.

  C She doesn't believe all of them.

  D She thinks they are exaggerated.

2 Why did the author start to eat Huel on the first evening?

  A She realised she hadn't been eating properly.

  B She recognised that she disliked cooking.

  C She didn't have time to prepare a meal.

  D She wasn't finding other foods satisfying.

3 What does 'these' in line 38 refer to?

  A unknown possible chemicals

  B lists on the label

  C other healthy meals

  D the main ingredients

4 What does the phrase 'got the hang of it' in line 40 mean?

  A was preparing to do something

  B learnt how to do something

  C got tired of doing something

  D realised she liked doing something

5 How did things change for the author in week two?

  A She started to do more exercise.

  B She gained a feeling of extra energy.

  C She wanted to give up her experiment.

  D She found what she ate more enjoyable.

6 At the end of the experiment, what did the author decide about Huel?

  A It was impossible to use it regularly.

  B She now knew how to use it properly.

  C It was a poor substitute for normal food.

  D Eating more of it would enable her to lose weight.

3 Complete sentences 1–7 with the correct form of the underlined words in the text.

1 They .... the old chef with a younger woman who had studied in Barcelona.

2 Apparently going on a juice fast can be ....

3 Vegetarianism is always a .... subject.

4 I'm less concerned about how food looks than how .... it is.

5 Lucy found giving up sugar a real ....

6 Orange juice .... the flavour of strawberries.

7 I was so .... in the TV programme *Master Chef* that I didn't hear the phone.

4 Match 1–6 with a–f to make collocations from the text.

1 maintain   **a** satisfied after a meal

2 tuck into   **b** a healthy weight

3 feel   **c** a meal filling

4 find   **d** calories

5 sip   **e** good food

6 count   **f** a drink

5 Read this report on the meal replacement industry. Cross out the option in italics that cannot be used.

The market for meal replacement drinks is **(1)** *raising/expanding/growing* very rapidly. This is because health care professionals have **(2)** *raised/grown/increased* our awareness of the dangers of overeating and because interest in keeping fit has **(3)** *grown/increased/raised* considerably. A person might decide to substitute one or more meals with a healthy shake and then **(4)** *increase/double/grow* their intake so that almost all meals are replaced. Apparently the numbers of people doing this have **(5)** *increased/grown/doubled* dramatically in the last six months. Many companies producing meal replacements are **(6)** *expanding/increasing/growing* production to meet the demand.

Grammar
passive forms
▶ CB page 54

1 **Find and correct the mistakes with passive forms in sentences 1–10.**

1 Rice is always serve with our meals.

2 Are you been picked up at the station?

3 Turkey are eaten every year at Christmas in the UK.

4 The cookery book was wrote by a famous television chef.

5 In the past, women was expected to do all the cooking.

6 Too much fast food are eaten nowadays.

7 It is believe that people should be educated about the health benefits of regular exercise.

8 People are expected throw their litter in the bins.

9 Orders for our banquet menu must placed in advance.

10 She was always being ask to prepare the food for parties.

2 **Complete the email with the correct active or passive form of the verbs in brackets.**

Dear Julia,

You'll never guess what **(1)** .... (*happen*). Our lovely new car **(2)** .... (*steal*)!

One day last week Jack went out to the beach for a swim and as usual he **(3)** .... (*hide*) the car keys in the toe of his shoe. When he came out of the water, he **(4)** .... (*not notice*) anything suspicious. It didn't look as if his clothes **(5)** .... (*touch*). When he started to put them on, however, he realised that the keys **(6)** .... (*take*) and when he got to the car park, of course, the car was gone too.

The police say there is a gang of car thieves who **(7)** .... (*know*) to be operating in the area. They think Jack **(8)** .... (*watch*) as he arrived at the beach. The thieves saw where he had parked the car and then where the keys **(9)** .... (*hide*).

It was almost two weeks ago now and although we hope it **(10)** .... (*find*), we're beginning to think we might never see it again.

Well, that's all from me. Write soon and tell me all your news.

Love,

Raquel

3 **Complete the second sentence so that it has a similar meaning to the first sentence, using the word given. Do not change the word given. You must use between two and five words, including the word given.**

1 The chef gave him the recipe.

WAS

He .... the chef.

2 The lecture about healthy food raised many interesting issues.

BROUGHT

Many interesting issues .... the lecture about healthy food.

3 Mary baked the cake using six eggs.

BAKED

The cake .... , who used six eggs.

4 You can't smoke anywhere in the restaurant.

PERMITTED

Smoking .... anywhere in the restaurant.

5 Please check that someone has washed up before you leave!

DONE

Please check that the .... before you leave.

6 Jo had opened the restaurant by himself before Rafa joined him as his business partner.

HAD

The restaurant .... Jo before Rafa joined him as his business partner.

Speaking
Long turn (Part 2)
▶ CB page 55

About the exam:

In the Speaking test, Part 2, each candidate is asked to compare two photographs and answer another question about them. The candidate talks about the photographs for about a minute, pointing out the similarities and differences between the photographs, and then answers the question which is also written above the photographs.

Strategy:

Make sure you leave enough time to answer the question after comparing the photographs.

1 ▶ 10 **Listen to the instruction an examiner gives to a candidate. What does the examiner ask the candidate to do?**

1 Compare the pictures and say how the people are feeling about being together.

2 Compare the photographs and say what the people are enjoying about eating in different places.

2 Complete the candidate's comparison of the two photographs with the words in the box.

clear	if	looks	obviously	
of	see	seems	shows	similar

Both these photographs are of people eating together. The first one **(1)** .... a barbecue. There are quite a lot of people so I think there must be more than one family involved. It **(2)** .... to be somewhere like the USA. There are a lot of trees in the background, and green grass. Everyone **(3)** .... as if they are really enjoying the barbecue and the pleasant landscape. There is a woman who is giving out food to the rest of her family and they are all smiling and laughing. I can **(4)** .... men who are standing around the barbecue, so I think they are still cooking. They're **(5)** .... just about to eat. The other photograph is **(6)** .... a family having breakfast. It's **(7)** .... to the first photograph in that everyone looks very happy and as **(8)** .... they are really enjoying being together. The older child is sitting down at a table and the younger child is sitting on her mother's lap. They are all sitting at one end of the table, which seems to make it easier for everyone to talk together and it's **(9)** .... that they are really enjoying that.

3 ▶ 11 Listen to a candidate giving her response to the photographs and complete her comments.

I think we all like joining our friends and family for meals **(1)** .... in the photos. It's particularly enjoyable to eat in the open air but even an ordinary meal **(2)** .... in the kitchen is a good time for the family to get together and talk before the beginning of a busy working day or at the weekends **(3)** ....

Writing
Review (Part 2)
▶ CB page 56

About the exam:
In Part 2 of the Writing paper, you choose to write one task from three options. One of these options might be a review.

Strategy:
- Balance your review by writing positive and negative comments on whatever the subject is.
- You can organise your comments into separate paragraphs (one for positive comments and one for negative) or combine them into one paragraph using linking words.

1 Look at this task and the points two students (A and B) plan to include. Which student's ideas will make a more interesting answer?

> You have been given this task by your English teacher.
>
> **Can you be our café critic?**
>
> Have you tried a new café near your school recently? We'd like to know about the food, the place itself and the cost. Tell us whether you would recommend it to other students.
>
> The best review will be published in the school newsletter.

A

Chill Out Natural Burger Bar

serves burgers and fruit juices

open every day

prices vary

only opened about six months ago

not popular with all my friends

cheap lunch

B

Gloria's Global Salad Bar

wide range of healthy options with vegetarian options

bright colours and posters on the walls

very busy so there can be queues – but worth it

friendly, helpful staff

rather loud music

some meals expensive, but there are cheap sandwiches and interesting salads

2 A review should include positive and negative points, although it should always give a final opinion. Which points in list B are negative?

3 Write your own review of Gloria's Salad Bar, using the points given. Decide whether your review is generally positive, and whether you would recommend the bar. Write 140–190 words.

6 In the spotlight

Speaking
Discussion (Part 4)
▶ CB page 58

1 ▶ 12 **Listen to two students completing a Part 4 task and decide if statements 1–8 are true (T) or false (F).**

1 The interlocutor in the first interview asks Ana about the difficulties of being a famous actor or musician.

2 Ana tries to include Mario in the discussion.

3 Mario summarises what Ana has said.

4 Ana does not accept Mario's argument.

5 The interlocutor in the second interview asks Celina for her opinions about the Eurovision Song Contest.

6 Celina tries to get Gabriel to express an opinion.

7 Gabriel summarises what Celina has said.

8 Gabriel agrees completely with Celina's opinion of the Eurovision Song Contest.

2 **Listen again and tick the phrases that you hear the candidates use.**

1 I think …

2 I see what you mean but …

3 Is that what you think too?

4 Would you agree?

5 In my opinion …

6 Well, I suppose you're right up to a point.

7 The point you're trying to make is …

8 What you're saying is …

9 I'm not sure about that.

10 As far as I'm concerned …

3 **Complete the table with the phrases from Activity 2.**

Expressing an opinion	Asking for the other candidate's opinion
(1)	(4) ....
(2)	(5) ....
(3)	
Tentatively disagreeing with the other candidate	**Summarising what the other candidate has said**
(6)	(9) ....
(7)	(10) ....
(8)	

Vocabulary
the arts ▶ CB page 59

1 Put the nouns in the box into the correct column. Some may go in more than one column.

actors   conductor   costumes   critics   director
exhibition   gallery   location   painting
performances   play   premiere   production
review   scenery   screenplay   set   stage

Film	Art	Theatre	Musical

2 Complete sentences 1–8 with words from Activity 1.

1 Have you seen the .... of the film online? The .... have been very complimentary about it.

2 I loved the film in general but the .... was very unnatural – the .... had difficulty saying the words.

3 The film was beautiful to look at – they filmed it on .... in the mountains.

4 That .... at the local art gallery is brilliant and there are some amazing paintings!

5 Last time I went to the theatre my seat was so far away from the .... I could hardly see what was happening! It was very cheap though.

6 I went to stand outside the cinema at the .... of the latest blockbuster film and I saw all the stars arriving, as well as the .... of the film.

7 I love musicals, but it's important to have a live orchestra – the .... makes such a difference to the way the music is played.

8 The last .... I saw at a theatre was by Shakespeare and the .... the actors wore were very traditional and from the right period so they looked great.

Listening
Multiple choice (Part 1) ▶ CB page 60

About the exam:
In the Listening paper, Part 1, you hear eight unrelated extracts. You answer one question about each extract by choosing from three options. You hear all the extracts twice.

Strategy:
• Read the question and all the options before you listen.
• After you have heard the extract, choose your answer, then move on to the next question.
• If you are not sure of an answer, don't worry about it – choose an option and move on.

1 ▶ 13 **You will hear people talking in eight different situations. For questions 1–8, choose the best answer (A, B or C).**

1 You hear two friends talking after an evening's entertainment. What did they see?
  A a film
  B a musical
  C a live performance

2 You hear a man talking about his choice of career. How does he feel about it?
  A sure that it is right for him
  B pleased to be following his parents' example
  C amused that his friends don't like what he does

3 You overhear a couple talking at a bus stop. How does the woman feel?
  A irritated by the man's attitude
  B worried about something else
  C frustrated by the situation

4 You hear part of a radio phone-in programme. Why has the man called the programme?
  A to complain about something
  B to clarify some facts
  C to make a suggestion

5 You hear a man talking about a television programme he is making. What is the focus of the programme?
  A improving public awareness of possible action
  B exposing the dangers of environmental problems
  C highlighting the difficulties of the environmental situation

6 You hear two friends talking about a film. What do they agree about the film?
  A The standard of acting was poor.
  B The special effects were disappointing.
  C The film was not as good as they'd expected.

7 You overhear two people talking. What is the relationship of the woman to the man?
  A line manager
  B wife
  C colleague

8 You hear a woman talking to a friend. What is she doing?
  A disagreeing with a point of view
  B recommending a solution to a situation
  C expressing regret about a mistake

Grammar
future forms
▶ CB page 61

1 **Complete sentences 1–8 with the correct future form of the verbs in brackets.**

1 I .... (*meet*) Jo outside the cinema at six – we arranged it this morning.

2 The plane .... (*leave*) at six, so I .... (*get*) a taxi to the airport at four probably.

3 That sounds like the postman; I .... (*check*) if he's left any post for you.

4 I'm not sure who'll win the gold medal; it .... (*be*) Magnus this year.

5 That new stadium is almost built – it's definitely .... (*finish*) next month.

6 I expect that the banks .... (*raise*) interest rates soon – that's what the papers say.

7 As soon as the programme .... (*end*), I'm going to bed.

8 We'll have dinner when Joe .... (*arrive*).

2 **Choose the correct phrases in italics to complete the dialogues.**

Dialogue 1

A: What **(1)** *are you doing/will you do* next year?

B: I **(2)** *'m studying/could study* acting at the Royal Academy of Dramatic Arts in London. I did an audition a while ago and I got an email to tell me I'd been accepted yesterday.

A: So you **(3)** *are going to live/live* in London?

B: Yes, **(4)** *I will/I am*. **(5)** *I'll probably share/I probably share* a flat with other students.

A: When **(6)** *does/will* the course start?

B: In mid-September but there **(7)** *will be/is going to be* an orientation week first.

A: Good luck with the course. I'm sure you **(8)** *will really enjoy/are really going to enjoy* it.

Dialogue 2

A: In what ways do you think the entertainment industry **(1)** *changes/will change* over the next few years?

B: Well, one thing I'm certain of is that things like CDs and DVDs **(2)** *are disappearing/will disappear* altogether. **(3)** *We'll download/We download* all of our music, movies and TV series directly from the internet.

C: Well, I agree that CDs **(4)** *are probably not going to be/are probably not* around for very much longer but I think the DVD boxed sets of TV series **(5)** *will still be/are still* popular, even if we can download everything we want. People find them very attractive. Some people are going back to vinyl LPs as well, so maybe **(6)** *there is/there'll be* a return to the good old days.

B: You could have a point there. Some people say that in fifty years' time no one **(7)** *will even remember/is remembering* what a printed book looks like and everyone **(8)** *reads/will read* on e-book readers or smartphones. But a lot of people like to hold a book in their hands and turn the pages.

Reading
Gapped text (Part 6)
▶ CB page 62

1 **You are going to read an article about film extras. Read the article and the sentences that have been removed (A–G) in Activity 2. Decide if the statements are true (T) or false (F).**

1 More film extras are used today than they were in the past.

2 You have to be special in some way to be a film extra.

2 **Read the article and the sentences that have been removed again. Choose from sentences A–G the one that fits each gap (1–6). There is one extra sentence which you do not need to use.**

A I learnt all this at first hand during my day as a supporting artist.

B These can look a bit fake.

C That's the life of an extra for you.

D It used to be a question of finding extras on the street and approaching the ones who looked right for a particular scene.

E Instead there was a lawyer, a banker and a music producer.

F I couldn't imagine why anyone would want to do this.

G They even have agents.

3 **Find words in the article connected with film and theatre to match definitions 1–6.**

1 the words of a speech or play that have been written down

2 the costume department or costumes of a theatre or film company

3 the person responsible for choosing the actors for a play or film

4 something built and decorated with furniture, scenery, etc. where actors perform part of a play/film

5 the part of a particular actor in a play or film

6 filming

LIFE AS A FILM EXTRA: HOLLYWOOD'S LEAST POWERFUL PEOPLE

The chariot race in the 1959 Roman epic *Ben Hur* will go down in history for two reasons. First, because 263 feet of film was shot for every one foot that made it into the final movie, making it the least economically shot section of any film. The second reason is that it features a trumpet-playing extra who forgot to take his watch off. The film won 11 Oscars, but 50 years later we still can't get past that one mistake. [1] Nobody notices you unless you do something wrong.

Little has changed since *Ben Hur*, apart from the fact that extras are now called 'supporting artists' but their 'artistry' begins and ends with walking, standing and sitting. It's rare for an extra to get to say anything so there are no lines to memorise and they seldom even see the script. [2] A week earlier, the assistant director of the film told me to turn up in a car park, at 7a.m., looking 'smart casual' and that in the scene in which I was supposed to act I should look 'happy'.

When I got there I saw production trailers, handling everything from wardrobe to catering and make-up. I was directed to a bus where extras wait until a member of the crew comes on board to choose people for particular scenes. The bus wasn't full of would-be actors as I had imagined. [3] They liked the idea of sitting on the bus and relaxing on their day off while earning a bit of extra cash.

The cost of extras is one of the reasons why epics such as *Ben Hur* are a thing of the past. Nowadays, where possible, crowds are digitised in. In *Gladiator*, they used 2,000 live actors to create a digital crowd of about 35,000 people. But for some of the crowd scenes, in addition to the real-life extras and the digital ones, they also used cut-outs made of cardboard. [4] Inflatable extras are more rounded and have the added advantage of being easy to deflate, store and reuse.

Even so, for the best human extras, there is still a wide variety of work. 'A casting director could be looking for five Spanish-speaking fire eaters in a circus scene, or 500 people to play zombies taking over a city,' says Jamie Howell, of extras agency Star Now. [5] The advent of the internet has made the whole casting process a lot easier.

It doesn't matter how old you are and it doesn't matter what you look like. In fact, the more ordinary you look, the better. Having George Clooneys or Angelina Jolies in the background is too distracting. Though there may be nothing distinctive about them, today's extras are real professionals and know their worth. [6] The extras I spoke to said this was the best way to get block bookings.

Finally, we were called on to the set for a fight scene. Our emotion as extras was 'surprise'. I was convinced that I was about to play my role brilliantly. Unfortunately, the scene didn't involve any extras in the end. We just had to watch them shooting it. But then the tea trolley arrived. Suddenly, I got it. All this, and biscuits too. The extra's life was starting to make sense.

4 Complete the tables with words from the article.

Adjective	Noun
mistaken	(1) ....
(2)	rarity
advantageous	(3) ....
(4)	width
emotional	(5) ....

Verb	Noun
(6)	memory
produce	(7) ....
(8)	choice
add	(9) ....
vary	(10) ....

5 Complete sentences 1–5 with words from Activity 4.

1 Only the best-known actors get to pick and .... the roles they take.

2 It was very moving to see the strong .... bond between the two dancers.

3 Finding someone who doesn't use any social media is a .... nowadays.

4 I've often been .... for George Clooney. I look exactly like him.

5 Having a good .... is often not regarded as important because technology does it all for us.

Grammar
future perfect and continuous
▶ CB page 64

1 There are words missing in some of the sentences below. Insert the words in the correct place. Tick the sentences that are correct.

By 2050 …

1 directors will started to make most of their films in places other than Hollywood.

2 everyone can already watch whatever they want via the internet, so soon DVDs have become redundant.

3 people won't have stopped going to big music festivals like Glastonbury and Benicassim every summer. They'll still be very popular.

4 many people will have stopped using mobile phones as a result of all the health warnings.

5 people will have using smartphone applications for so long that they'll have got bored with them.

6 webcams will have become 3D so that it will really feel as if the person you are talking to is in the room with you.

7 a lot of record companies will have gone out of business because most people have started to make their own music and upload it to the internet.

8 people will got used to paying for music and will accept this as only right and fair since the money will go directly to the performer.

Use of English
Multiple-choice cloze (Part 1)
▶ CB page 65

1 Match questions 1–6 with answers A–F.

1 Is there anything you don't get about the homework?

2 Can you get your parents to do whatever you want?

3 When did you last get really angry?

4 How do you get to school every day?

5 How many cups of coffee do you get through in a day?

6 How tired do you get at the end of the day?

A Oh yes – I just have to be nice to them.

B I'm not sure about the writing task.

C Not very – I often go to the gym then.

D I'm actually trying to cut down!

E By bus, unless dad takes me in the car.

F It must have been when my mobile phone was stolen.

2 Choose the correct preposition in italics to complete the sentences.

1 It took me ages to get *over/through* that virus but I'm better now.

2 I can't come out tonight because I've got too much work to get *off/through*.

3 Bad weather always gets me *under/down*; I feel much happier when the sun shines!

4 I hate ironing so I just leave it and never get *round to/in to* doing it.

5 My boss is really tough so I never get *over with/away with* poor-quality work.

6 I really got *into/up* skiing last winter; I loved it and want to go again!

7 I love chocolate but I'm trying to cut *down/off* on the amount I eat every day, otherwise I'll get fat!

8 I work hard so holidays are important to me – I try to get *away/through* at least twice a year.

3 For questions 1–8, read the text and decide which word (A, B, C or D) best fits each gap.

To be a star or not to be a star?

If you're longing to lead a film-star lifestyle, join the queue of hundreds of would-be actors streaming into Hollywood, **(0)** _D. heading_ for the movie studios where they think their dreams will come **(1)** .... But it goes without **(2)** .... that virtually none of these hopefuls will go straight into major roles in mainstream films. Most find temporary jobs to pay the rent, waiting for the **(3)** .... break they think will come eventually – though the **(4)** .... are heavily stacked against them. It isn't easy to get yourself invited to any kind of **(5)** .... Even if you do, being rejected is part of the process – you have to get **(6)** .... it and keep on trying. Never let it get you **(7)** .... – if you do, you will never succeed. Having said that, you should have an alternative plan just in case you don't **(8)** .... it to the top. If you have to accept that your dreams are just that, and do something completely different, it may actually turn out to be ultimately more satisfying.

0	**A** going	**B** getting	**C** setting	**D** heading
1	**A** true	**B** correct	**C** right	**D** real
2	**A** speaking	**B** saying	**C** talking	**D** expressing
3	**A** huge	**B** big	**C** enormous	**D** massive
4	**A** chances	**B** opportunities	**C** odds	**D** gains
5	**A** audition	**B** rehearsal	**C** practice	**D** interview
6	**A** to	**B** under	**C** through	**D** over
7	**A** down	**B** off	**C** on	**D** in
8	**A** succeed	**B** make	**C** get	**D** pass

Writing
Report (Part 2)
▶ CB page 66

About the exam:
In Part 2 of the Writing paper, you may choose to write a report. You will be given some information and ideas about what to write.

Strategy:
Read the instructions and the whole task very carefully. Identify:
- the purpose of your report.
- what you have to write about.

You should evaluate your ideas and make recommendations or give your opinion at the end. Use a semi-formal style.

1 You see this announcement on your school noticeboard.

We want your ideas!
We are planning to set up a performing arts club for students, which could include a choir, dance group or theatre group.

Which of these ideas would students like most? How can we improve the facilities that are already there?

Send us a report and we will make a decision.

Write your report in 140–190 words.

2 Look at the DOs and DON'Ts and the report a student wrote. Put a cross (✗) next to advice he has ignored and a tick (✓) next to advice he has followed.

1 ☐ DO give your report a heading.
2 ☐ DON'T begin 'Dear Sir or Madam'.
3 ☐ DO divide your report into clear sections.
4 ☐ DO use headings which link to the task.
5 ☐ DON'T give your opinion at the beginning.
6 ☐ DON'T use very informal language.
7 ☐ DO use an impersonal style, e.g. the passive and reporting verbs (it was suggested/claimed/believed).
8 ☐ DO use expressions of purpose, linkers and quantity expressions such as quite a few, several.
9 ☐ DO check spelling carefully.
10 ☐ DO make recommendations.

This report is to sugest ways in wich we could establish a performing arts club in our school. I interveved a number of students about this issue and the following were there oppinions. Most students were in favour of forming a choir. It was felt that almost everyone would enjoy this. Although it was acknowledged that singing ability varies, it was generally aggreed that in a large group individual talent was not a problem. Another opinion that was shared among the students was that the music chosen should be mostly rock or pop music rather than clasical. Beatles songs were often mentioned in the survey as were Abba and Take That. Finally, a number of students raised the issue of rehersal space and equipment. Although the common room is the obvious place to rehearse, it was pointed out that the piano needs to be repairred. In my opinion a choir offers students an excellent way of taking part in performing arts, and the piano should be repaird.

3 Write the report out again following the advice in Activity 2 that the student ignored.

4 Now write your own answer to the task.

Multiple-choice cloze (Part 1)

For questions 1–8, read the text below and decide which answer (A, B, C or D) best fits each gap. There is an example at the beginning (0).

Do men really cook better than women?

Are women better cooks than men because they have a natural love for food and don't show **(0)** *B off* ? Or are men better because they **(1)** .... cooking more seriously? Maybe it has **(2)** .... to do with nature – women may be more instinctive, have a better **(3)** .... of smell and a greater understanding of food. **(4)** .... , there are other things to take into account when considering cooking as a career.

Restaurant kitchens are still a man's world. Yet, **(5)** .... the fact that the work is physical and stressful, women are calmer in the kitchen, and often have a different attitude; they cook to show they enjoy **(6)** .... care of others. As one said, '**(7)** .... I'd love to run my own restaurant, and I'm sure it would be very rewarding, but I'd **(8)** .... teach people to be good home cooks. That's the way to create a love of cooking in future generations.'

0	**A** out	**B** off	**C** in	**D** up
1	**A** take	**B** hold	**C** think	**D** have
2	**A** nothing	**B** some	**C** anything	**D** none
3	**A** instinct	**B** feeling	**C** sense	**D** touch
4	**A** Moreover	**B** In addition	**C** Also	**D** However
5	**A** in spite	**B** though	**C** despite	**D** whether
6	**A** giving	**B** looking	**C** making	**D** taking
7	**A** Conversely	**B** Fortunately	**C** Naturally	**D** Hopefully
8	**A** prefer	**B** better	**C** rather	**D** fairly

Open cloze (Part 2)

For questions 9–16, read the text below and think of the word which best fits each gap. Use only one word in each gap. There is an example at the beginning (0).

A good show? Really?

I love going to the theatre but I am often disappointed **(0)** *by* the show itself, which fails to live **(9)** .... to my expectations. So what's the best way to **(10)** .... out whether a particular production is worth seeing? Some people read the critical reviews, but **(11)** .... far can they be trusted? There are always glowing tributes outside theatres promising a 'thrilling' evening, or a 'sensational' show, but many theatre managers choose these advertising quotations **(12)** .... great care. This is because they want to **(13)** .... theatre-goers the impression that the reviews were **(14)** .... positive than they might have been. One musical was advertised with the words 'the songs remind you of how fabulous the band were', but more negative comments were left **(15)** .... So maybe what we have to do **(16)** .... read the reviews carefully, but then trust our own judgement about whether we should pay good money to go and see the show.

Word formation (Part 3)

For questions 17–24, read the text below. Use the word given in capitals at the end of some of the lines to form a word that fits in the gap in the same line. There is an example at the beginning (0).

The problem of plastic

It seems to have become **(0)** _acceptable_ to carry plastic water bottles everywhere. Although it's claimed that these contain pure water transported from isolated glaciers or springs, as a concept it's both **(17)** .... , and expensive.

ACCEPT

RIDICULE

Yet attitudes may be changing, driven not by the **(18)** .... of simply being seen to drink water advertised as 'pure', but by evidence of the damage plastic bottles are doing to our environment. Apart from the **(19)** .... litter created by discarded bottles on roadsides or beaches, tiny plastic particles almost **(20)** .... to the human eye get into our oceans. These are eaten by fish, which are caught and cooked in restaurants. As a consequence, when we enjoy a fish meal we may be eating plastic too.

STUPID

PLEASE

VISIBLE

We need to raise everyone's **(21)** .... of the importance of avoiding plastic, but **(22)** .... education takes time. Meanwhile we should avoid **(23)** .... trends like bottled water, for the sake of our own health and that of the planet. **(24)** .... it's the responsible thing to do.

AWARE

UNIVERSE

FASHION

CLEAR

Key word transformation (Part 4)

For questions 25–30, complete the second sentence so that it has a similar meaning to the first sentence, using the word given. Do not change the word given. You must use between two and five words, including the word given. Here is an example (0).

Example:

0 A very kind friend took us home after the party.

TAKEN

After the party, we _were taken home by_ a very kind friend.

25 I couldn't wait to see my friend again after her long trip abroad.

LOOKING

I .... my friend again after her long trip abroad.

26 The last time Joe saw Carlos was the day they both graduated from university.

SEEN

Carlos .... the day they both graduated from university.

27 'You must do your homework, Tom,' said Carol.

REMINDED

Carol .... his homework.

28 I never seem to find the time to read newspapers these days.

ROUND

I never seem to .... newspapers these days.

29 Nothing irritates me as much as getting piles of junk mail through the post.

MORE

There is nothing .... getting piles of junk mail through the post.

30 The idea of flying is very frightening for some people.

ARE

Some people .... the idea of flying.

7 A place to live

Vocabulary
expressions with *home*

1 **Complete the sentences with the expressions in the box.**

| at home | feel at home | holiday home | home from home |
| home town | stay at home | | |

1 I was born and brought up in Paris – that's my ....
2 George is a very good host – he makes everyone .... in his house.
3 I'm saving to buy a .... ; somewhere I can go to every summer.
4 I can't afford to go away this summer – I'm going to ....
5 Oh no – I haven't got my wallet with me. I must have left it ....
6 Every time I go to Barcelona I stay with my friends Eva and Josep. Their house has become a real .... for me.

Reading
Multiple matching (Part 7)
▶ CB page 70

1 **You are going to read an article about a woman who lives on a canal boat. Read the article quickly and decide if the following statement is true or false.**

Helen is thinking about moving because living on a boat can be difficult.

2 **Read the article again. For questions 1–10, choose from the sections (A–D). The sections may be chosen more than once.**

Which paragraph

explains that more than one type of person joins a boating community?	1
describes how Helen's and her boyfriend's way of life fits their values?	2
indicates the time Helen has spent living on the boat already?	3
gives the reason Helen wanted to change the way she lived before?	4
mentions that Helen and her boyfriend are more conscious of the resources they use?	5
describes how Helen prepared herself to live on a boat?	6
mentions something that Helen didn't know before she started living on a boat?	7
describes some benefits the boats have for the wider community?	8
explains why Helen couldn't buy a house?	9
points out that the material the boat is made of can be a problem?	10

Why I swapped bricks and mortar for a houseboat

Helen Babbs calls the canals her home

A It's a chilly February morning and I'm struggling to get out of bed. That period of time between pulling back the covers and the cabin heating up is tough to step into. So I lie still, listening to a chorus of creaking rope, slapping water and shouting <u>coots</u>. It has been a hard night. I got in late after dinner with friends and didn't light a fire, or even fill a hot-water bottle. I brushed my teeth still in my coat. The cold <u>crept</u> in overnight, so piercing that it woke me up: a reminder that my home is made of steel and partly submerged in water. Unless the fire is lit, the cabin temperature can go down dramatically when it's cool out. Even though I was doing that only three years ago, it's hard to remember what it's like to wake up on dry land.

B I moved to the boat the year I turned 30. After 10 years of renting rooms in shared flats, I was desperate for a space with only me and my boyfriend in it. Buying a flat or house is far wiser, but self-employed, low-earning writers like me don't get mortgages easily – and we live in London, where £450,000 is the starting price for a home. That isn't to say living on the water is cheap – boats can cost tens of thousands, plus there are yearly licence fees, insurance and fuel costs. And expenses can <u>spiral</u> if you include maintenance work. But living afloat was a dream we'd long had. We researched it heavily, and I stayed on a friend's boat for a month to learn the ropes. We found our boat in Derbyshire – she's plain on the outside but her cabin is lovely: all oak, pine and brass. We bought her <u>outright</u> for under £70,000. Handing over the money was both terrifying and thrilling. We both knew we still had a lot to learn.

C The boat allows us to live in tune with things we care about – respecting the environment, living sustainably. We have solar panels and a cast-iron stove, our main source of heat. Life on the boat has made us much more <u>conservative</u> about how much power and water we use but that's actually surprisingly liberating. We're also close to nature – sharing the canal with cormorants and herons, grey wagtails and pipistrelle bats. London's waterways are home to a growing number of boats. The people who live on them aren't just hippies; they're just decent folk finding creative ways to live. Our neighbours can be families, couples or friends sharing, or people on their own. It's a low-impact community worth <u>celebrating</u>. Boats bring colour and character to modern cities, which are often rather <u>sterile</u>.

D Still, it's important not to romanticise. Residential <u>moorings</u> are scarce and many boaters have to move their boats every two weeks. Without a permanent address, banking and healthcare become complicated. For many, seeing a doctor is difficult without proof of a permanent address. It was a shock to discover I had to register as homeless if I wanted to vote. We've also had to put up with some occasional antisocial <u>antics</u> – it's rare but we've found strangers on our roof at 4a.m. But, despite all this, my boat is my home. I have no plans to <u>retreat</u> to dry land.

3 Look at the underlined words in the article and match 1–6 to the best meaning, A or B.

1 coots
   A water birds
   B old men you think are strange or unpleasant

2 crept
   A moved in a quiet and careful way to avoid attracting attention
   B gradually filled

3 spiral
   A move in a continuous curve
   B increase quickly

4 outright
   A completely, having paid the full price
   B clearly and directly

5 conservative
   A careful
   B old-fashioned

6 celebrating
   A praising
   B rejoicing

7 sterile
   A completely clean
   B not interesting or attractive

8 moorings
   A the ropes or chains that fasten a boat to the land or the bottom of the sea
   B the places where boats are fastened to the land

9 antics
   A adventures
   B silly or annoying behaviour

10 retreat
   A go away to a place that is safe
   B ignore what is happening around you

Grammar

modal verbs
▶ CB page 72

1 Complete the sentences with the correct form of the modal verbs in the box. Make any other necessary changes. You can use the words more than once.

can	could	may	might	must

1 The test wasn't so bad – it .... a lot worse!

2 I haven't seen her today so she .... ill, though it's unlikely.

3 Sue hasn't replied to my email which is not like her; she .... received it.

4 He .... here because he sent me a text to tell me he'd arrived in the building.

5 I didn't hear the postman knock – I .... asleep.

6 I drove to work but I can't find my car keys now. I .... left them in my coat pocket – I often do!

2 Write sentences similar in meaning to sentences 1–6. Use one of the modal verbs in brackets to replace the underlined words and phrases.

1 I don't know why I can't contact her – it's possible her mobile phone is switched off. (*must/could*)

2 He <u>has</u> his own webpage, <u>I'm pretty sure</u>. (*may/must*)

3 <u>It's impossible for them to</u> be eating outside because it's raining! (*can't/mustn't*)

4 <u>It's possible that</u> John <u>is</u> arriving tonight. (*might/must*)

5 <u>It's impossible for us to</u> leave because it's too early. (*couldn't/can't*)

6 <u>I'm not sure, but I think that</u> the new student <u>is</u> from Germany. (*could/must*)

Speaking

Long turn (Part 2)
▶ CB page 73

1 ▶ 14 Listen to an interlocutor giving a candidate instructions about the two photographs. What does the interlocutor ask the candidate to do?

1 Compare the photographs and say why people have chosen to celebrate their weddings in these situations.

2 Compare the photographs and say which of these weddings would be more difficult to organise.

2 Decide whether phrases 1–10 express certainty (C) or probability (P).

1 They seem/appear (to be) …

2 It looks like/as if (they are) …

3 It/They must be/have done …

4 It/They could/may be/have done …

5 It/They can't be/have done …

6 I imagine (that they are) …

7 I'm fairly/absolutely certain (they are) …

8 As far as I can see, (they are) …

9 I suppose (they are) …

10 They are definitely …

3 ▶ 15 Listen to what a candidate said about the photos in Activity 1 and complete the text.

Well, the first couple have chosen to have a cycling wedding. **(1)** .... they are on their way to the reception in the photograph and that the wedding ceremony itself **(2)** .... already taken place. **(3)** .... very happy about it, and the other members of the wedding party **(4)** .... they are enjoying it too. The other couple have decided to have one of their wedding photos taken under water. **(5)** .... have had the actual wedding there. **(6)** .... of that.

The first couple **(7)** .... cycling fanatics. **(8)** .... really love the sport if they have chosen to cycle to the reception. The other couple **(9)** .... just wanted an unusual wedding photograph for their wedding album. **(10)** .... an underwater photograph would be rather difficult to take but it **(11)** .... be fun. **(12)** .... there's nobody else in the photo, so **(13)** .... it was also taken after the wedding itself. **(14)** .... been taken the day after. It wouldn't be much fun sitting through the reception in a wet wedding dress!

Listening
Multiple choice (Part 4)
▶ CB page 74

1 The words in the box are used to describe places. Which two are positive?

characterless	desolate	empty
grandeur	remarkable	weird

2 ▶ 16 **You will hear a radio interview with a musician and photographer called Karen Wilson. For questions 1–7, choose the best answer (A, B or C).**

1 What does Karen say about her teachers at school?

  A They developed her interest in music.

  B They enabled her to improve her artistic talent.

  C They followed old-fashioned methods of teaching.

2 How did Karen feel when she was asked to write a travel book?

  A concerned about other people seeing her pictures

  B pleased to be able to demonstrate her individuality

  C surprised that a publisher was interested in her

3 In her books, Karen's main aim is to

  A encourage more people to travel widely.

  B help people enjoy their own travel experiences.

  C make people think more deeply about what they see.

4 Karen says that what she finds fascinating about places is

  A the mismatch between appearance and reality.

  B the different types of place she has to go to.

  C the different people she meets on her travels.

5 What did Karen enjoy most about her trip to Argentina?

  A seeing unusual wildlife

  B giving successful concerts

  C being alone in the natural landscape

6 What does Karen say she has learnt from travelling?

  A It can be fun to see as many places as possible.

  B It's sometimes necessary to accept places for what they are.

  C It improves the experience if you try to understand a place.

7 What does Karen say has contributed most to her success?

  A having a lot of luck in life

  B responding to a challenge

  C getting support from others

Vocabulary
travel: collocations and phrasal verbs
▶ CB page 75

1 Complete the sentences with the words in the box.

business trip	camping trip	domestic flights
guided tour	package holiday	return ticket
season ticket	sightseeing tour	

1 I'm looking forward to the .... of the city – it's the best way to see a lot of places in a short time.

2 Buy a .... for the train because two singles are much more expensive.

3 I'm going on a .... to the mountains with friends – it's great to live rough!

4 People who commute to the city from the country buy an annual .... for the train.

5 .... within a country are usually cheaper than international flights.

6 My husband is going on a .... to Germany, but I'm not going because he'll be working all the time.

7 I went on a .... of Windsor Castle and learnt so much about the history of the place from the expert who showed us round.

8 When you book a .... everything is organised including accommodation and travel.

2 Complete the phrasal verbs in the sentences.

1 Most people like to get .... for a short holiday every year.

2 I prefer to stay with a friend who can put me .... instead of checking .... to a hotel.

3 I always set .... in plenty of time in case I get held .... by traffic on my way to the airport.

4 I often leave things .... when I travel – I'm very forgetful!

5 I never plan a holiday – I like to turn .... at the airport and just choose where to go.

Grammar

relative clauses
▶ CB page 76

1 **Underline the correct relative pronouns in italics.**

1 I don't enjoy stories *that/who* have sad endings.

2 The island, *which/that* is smaller than Wales, is very beautiful.

3 The city, *who's/whose* main industry is tourism, is growing bigger every year.

4 Most tourists *which/who* come to the island choose the summer months.

5 It's July and August *when/where* the temperatures are warmest.

6 The place *that/where* you can see a glorious sunset is on the beach.

7 Tourists often want to visit the caves, in *where/which* you can see amazing wall paintings.

8 All the tourist guides, *who/that* speak many languages, are extremely good.

9 It's the food they cook on the barbecue *where/that* is my favourite.

10 I'm not sure *whose/who's* coming to the party but I know there will be a lot of people.

2 **Do the sentences in Activity 1 contain defining (D) or non-defining (ND) relative clauses?**

Use of English

Key word transformation (Part 4)
▶ CB page 77

1 **Complete the second sentence so that it has a similar meaning to the first sentence, using the word given. Do not change the word given. You must use between two and five words, including the word given. Here is an example (0).**

0 It seems as though they have cancelled the meeting.
   LIKE
   It looks like the meeting has been cancelled.

1 I think I'm too impatient to be a teacher.
   ENOUGH
   I don't think _____ to be a teacher.

2 Because I was really enjoying the trip I didn't want it to end.
   MUCH
   I was enjoying the trip _____ I didn't want it to end.

3 I couldn't understand the lecture because it was so technical.
   FOR
   The lecture was _____ to understand.

4 It was the most exciting film I have ever seen.
   NEVER
   I have _____ exciting film before.

5 It's possible that you met him at the party but it seems unlikely.
   COULD
   You _____ at the party but it seems unlikely.

6 I think she is definitely telling us the truth.
   LYING
   She _____ to us.

Writing

Essay (Part 1)
▶ CB page 78

1 **Read the exam task and answer the question below.**

In your English class you have been talking about why people choose to travel abroad. Now, your teacher has asked you to write an essay.

> There is no need for people to travel to find out about the world when they can see it all on the internet. What's your opinion?
>
> **Notes**
> Write about:
> 1 personal experience
> 2 languages
> 3 _____ (your own idea)

What could 'your own idea' be? Mark the one that would not be appropriate to include in the essay.

A having fun

B saving money

C having good wifi connection

D becoming more confident

2 Read the essay below and match paragraphs 2, 3 and 4 to the topics in the task in Activity 1.

People travel abroad for many reasons, but <u>the most likely</u> reason is for a holiday. However, is this really necessary now that we can all see everything about the world through the internet?

.... <u>I believe that</u> there is nothing better than personal experience. People can see a beautiful place on their computer, <u>but</u> they can't hear the birds, smell the flowers or get a true feeling about it.

.... <u>Another factor is</u> being able to speak to local people in their own language. <u>Of course</u> it's possible to learn other languages in your own country, and even on the internet itself, but if you can speak to people in their own country, it gives you confidence and you find out more about them. It can also be great fun.

.... <u>Finally</u>, and <u>to put a different point of view</u>, I would say that using the internet is the best way of finding a lot of information about a place if you can't visit it yourself, and it's certainly true that it is much cheaper than actually travelling.

<u>However</u> in brief, there is no doubt that travelling is the best thing and everyone should do it.

3 What are the reasons the writer gives for his/ her opinions? Tick those that are mentioned.

Paragraph 2
- [ ] having a real experience
- [ ] not being able to see everything
- [ ] not seeing wildlife

Paragraph 3
- [ ] being able to learn
- [ ] having fun
- [ ] meeting other people

Paragraph 4
- [ ] finding facts
- [ ] saving time
- [ ] cost

4 In which paragraph could the following reasons also be included?

a .... being able to take photographs
b .... convenience
c .... helping with future job prospects
d .... having memories
e .... getting more independent
f .... helping the environment

5 Look at paragraphs 1 and 5 in the essay in Activity 2. Match them to the functions below. There is one you don't need to use.

a .... to introduce the general topic
b .... to give the writer's own opinion
c .... to give reasons for the writer's opinion

6 Tick the words and phrases below that could be used instead of the underlined words in the essay in Activity 2. You might need to change some other words in the essay to make the substitution.

1 the most likely
   a possibly b conversely c probably
2 I believe that
   a In my opinion b It is common knowledge
   c It's often said
3 but
   a since b although c unless
4 Another factor is
   a However b In addition c Nevertheless
5 Of course
   a Clearly b Really c Actually
6 Finally
   a At last b In the end c Lastly
7 to put a different point of view
   a against b the opposite c on the other hand
8 However
   a Conversely b Well c To sum up

7 Now write your own answer to the exam task below. Remember to think of good reasons for your opinions and to use a variety of linking words. Write 140–190 words.

In your English class you have been talking about working in another country. Now, your teacher has asked you to write an essay.

Is it a good idea for young people to spend a short time working or studying abroad?

Notes
Write about:
1 personal experience
2 languages
3 .... (your own idea)

8 Moving on

Listening
Multiple matching (Part 3)
▶ CB page 80

1 **Match expressions 1–5 to meanings A–E.**

1	be top of my list	**A**	start something
2	take the first steps	**B**	relax
3	earn big money	**C**	investigate
4	go into something	**D**	have a good salary
5	chill (with friends)	**E**	be most important

2 ▶ **17 You will hear five different people talking about jobs they plan to do in the future. Choose from the list (A–H) the reason each speaker gives for wanting to do the job. There are three extra letters which you do not need to use.**

A the influence of friends

B following a parent's example

C pursuing a dream

D the potential salary

E a desire to travel

F good prospects for promotion

G wanting to combine a hobby with work

H the chance to meet people

Speaker 1 [ ]

Speaker 2 [ ]

Speaker 3 [ ]

Speaker 4 [ ]

Speaker 5 [ ]

Vocabulary
collocations and phrasal verbs with *work*
▶ CB page 81

1 **Read the clues and do the crossword.**

Across

2 Nursing used to be considered a female …

4 work out (in a gym)

6 He got his job through an employment …

7 I've always wanted to be a personal … and help people get fit.

8 There are a lot of … opportunities in engineering.

Down

1 worked up (about an upsetting incident)

3 work out (the cost of something)

5 Acting is great but there's no job …

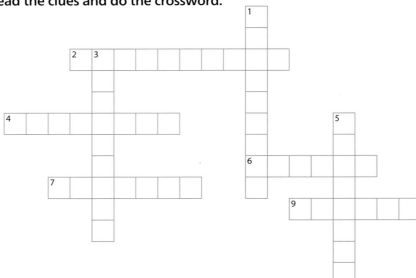

2 Choose the correct preposition in italics to complete the phrasal verbs.

1 Some people get worked *out/up* before an exam.

2 It's not always easy to work *around/down* problems.

3 It's great when new jobs work *out/off* really well.

Speaking
Collaborative task (Part 3)
▶ CB page 82

1 Look at the speaking task and the discussion that two students had about it. Complete the discussion using words from the box.

> Here are some things that people often think are important when they work from home. Talk together about whether these things are important for people who work from home.

different types of communication

fast internet connection

Are these things important for people who work from home?

separate room as office

opportunities to relax

contact with other people

---

colleagues   concentrate   deadlines
desk   desktop   distraction   landline
self-disciplined

A = Ana, M = Marek, I = Interlocutor

A: Well, if you work at home, I imagine it's important to have contact with other people.

M: <u>I suppose so.</u> If you don't have any **(1)** .... to talk to, you need other people around or you get lonely.

A: It's good to have a bit of company but the trouble with friends and relatives in the house is they can be a bit of a **(2)** .... The television's the same, especially if they want to have it on all the time.

M: You need a separate office. After all, if you're working you need to be able to **(3)** .... I know I'd be tempted to do other things – I'd take every opportunity to relax!

A: <u>That's just what I was going to say.</u> You need to get away if you want to focus, though it's also important to take breaks.

M: <u>It goes without saying that</u> a computer's absolutely essential.

A: But <u>actually I'm not sure it's necessary</u> to have a **(4)** .... computer. Maybe a laptop would be better. Then you can work anywhere you want.

M: <u>That's true</u> but I'm not very **(5)** .... and on sunny days I'd probably be relaxing in the garden instead of getting my work done.

A: Ah, but <u>that's why it'd be important</u> to have a schedule to keep track of your **(6)** ....

M: <u>What about different types of communication?</u> I wouldn't want a telephone on my **(7)** .... if I were working at home. There'd be too many interruptions.

A: Well, you probably don't need a **(8)** .... if you've got a mobile, but <u>you certainly need a fast internet connection.</u>

I: Now decide which one is *not* important for people who work from home.

A: <u>I guess for me it's</u> between opportunities to relax and contact with other people. <u>What do you think?</u>

M: <u>I'd probably go along with that.</u> There's an argument for different types of communication as well, though. I'd probably choose contact with other people – after all, you speak to people when you contact them – and work is work, not a social occasion.

A: I see what you mean.

2 Put the underlined expressions from Activity 1 into the correct section of the table.

Agreeing
(1) ....
(2) ....
(3) ....
(4) ....
Asking for an opinion
(5) ....
(6) ....
Expressing opinions
(7) ....
(8) ....
(9) ....
(10) ....
(11) ....

Grammar
reporting verbs
▶ CB page 83

1 There are mistakes in some of the sentences below. Find and correct the mistakes and tick the sentences that are correct.

0 Andrew asked me whether I ~~will~~ *would* finish the report by Friday.

1 Carlos told that he would meet us at the cinema.

2 Harry offered giving me a lift to the station.

3 Joe reminded me to call the hotel to cancel the reservation.

4 The boss accused me using the internet at work.

5 We warned him to avoid the traffic jam in Port Street.

6 Sue suggested us to take the bus because the trains were running late.

7 Juan explained that the computer system had crashed so emails weren't getting through.

8 Peter refused apologising to Mary.

2 For questions 1–6, complete the second sentence so that it has a similar meaning to the first sentence, using the word given. Do not change the word given. You must use between two and five words, including the word given.

0 'Can you lend me your car, Lee?' asked Chris.

BORROW

Chris asked *Lee if he could borrow* his car.

1 'I don't think you should go out without an umbrella,' said Jaime.

ADVISED

Jaime .... go out without an umbrella.

2 'I didn't write that bad report,' he said.

DENIED

He .... that bad report.

3 'Send Bob a card – it's his birthday on Friday,' said mum.

REMINDED

Mum .... a card because it was his birthday on Friday.

4 'Don't be late to work tomorrow,' the boss told us.

WARNED

The boss .... late to work the next day.

5 'You should take more exercise,' said the doctor.

RECOMMENDED

The doctor .... more exercise.

6 'I'll help you with that report,' said Karen.

OFFERED

Karen .... with the report.

Reading
Multiple matching (Part 7)
▶ CB page 84

1 You are going to read an article about four people who work from home. Read the article once quickly and decide which of these two sentences would make the best introduction to the article.

A Susan Taylor tells us about four people who disliked going out to work so much that they decided to stay at home.

B Susan Taylor talks to four people about the disadvantages of working from home.

2 Find the underlined words and phrases in the article and match them to the correct meaning, A or B.

1 breathing down your neck (line 3)

  A constantly watching what you do

  B standing too close to you

2 lifeline (line 14)

  A a kind of telephone line

  B something that makes it possible for you to survive

3 established (line 17)

  A recognised and accepted

  B conservative

4 squished (line 23)

  A seated on soft cushions

  B between people who are pushing against you

5 switch off (line 27)

  A stop a machine working

  B stop thinking about work

6 ungodly (line 33)

  A very early

  B not religious

7 dodgy (line 59)

  A exciting

  B low quality

When you don't go out to work

A Max: language tutor

My work involves teaching people English via the internet. The best thing about working from home is not having anyone <u>breathing down your neck</u> or telling you what to do and being able to work in your own time. I teach
5 people in other time zones **so** a lot of my classes are in the evenings or early mornings. The negative points have to be when an unexpected caller insists on ringing the doorbell when I'm working or when it's a very hot, sunny day and you'd rather be out in the sunshine but have to
10 put in your hours. At the beginning, I was putting in far too many hours, actually. That was before I started using a diary. I make a hand-written note of all my appointments and classes, personal and professional alike. It's my <u>lifeline</u>. I have one unbreakable rule, though: I always keep
15 Sunday free for myself.

B Peter: historian

I have always been home-based. Soon after university I started work as a researcher for an <u>established</u> writer on archaeology and then I started writing my own books. Of course, I have had other jobs. As a kid I used to help in
20 my parents' shop and I had a few holiday office jobs as a student **as well**. What I learnt from that was I never wanted to do that sort of thing again! I feel sorry for those people who spend two hours a day <u>squished</u> in a Tube train breathing in bad air and then have to work in places
25 like that. My office at home, the largest room in the house, has a sofa, TV and radio. I think it is important to be able to <u>switch off</u> occasionally and watch the news or whatever. Apart from not having to travel every day, you can also do two things at the same time, like monitoring the washing
30 machine while getting on with work.

C Mervin: musical supplier

I supply music rolls for mechanical organs. For me working from home has all the usual advantages like not having to get up at some <u>ungodly</u> hour to go out to work, especially when it's freezing outside; no office politics, no
35 boss looking over my shoulder and I can sit in the garden with my wife when the sun comes out. I can't think of any disadvantages **but** there are some things to take into account. Firstly, a home-based business sometimes has less credibility than a 'proper' one. It's generally not a good
40 idea to let new customers know that you are working from home until you can show them that you are serious about what you do. **Another thing is that** sometimes it is illegal to run a business from your premises unless you get planning permission, especially if your work involves extra
45 traffic, either deliveries or people, activity or noise.

D Gary: magazine journalist

I was injured in a car crash and was stuck in the house with nothing to do. I did a lot of thinking about things and realised that I hated my job so much that it was making me miserable. **Despite** having wanted to be a
50 journalist since I was a kid, I'd never really tried to get into it. It seemed a good time to change that, so I decided to contact a magazine with some story ideas. I ended up with my first commission and had enough work to go self-employed within six months. I need to do things pretty much the minute I get the commission. I don't mind,
55 **though**. I like the pressure. I do find that without it, I just don't work. I need to have a bit of a crisis mentality. That's where I get the motivation from. Without it I end up watching <u>dodgy</u> television programmes instead of working.
60

---

3 **Read the article again. For questions 1–10, choose from the people A–D.**

Which person

offers advice about running a business from home?	**1**
finds it annoying when others interrupt his work?	**2**
had to control the time he was spending on work?	**3**
sometimes finds self-discipline a problem?	**4**
regards taking breaks and relaxing as a good thing?	**5**
likes to spend longer in bed in the mornings?	**6**
resists the temptation to go and sit outside?	**7**
sympathises with people who have to commute?	**8**
has managed to fulfil an ambition?	**9**
relies on an old-fashioned way of organising things?	**10**

4 **Complete the paragraph with the words and phrases in bold in the article in Activity 2.**

I work in the evenings from five to ten. I don't mind, **(1)** .... It means I don't have to get up early in the morning. **(2)** .... if I have to do something like go to the bank or the dentist, I don't have to take time off work. I can do all my shopping in the mornings **(3)** .... My girlfriend is a student and her classes are in the mornings **(4)** .... we don't get to see much of each other during the week. That's a pity **(5)** .... it can't be helped. **(6)** .... not getting home until about 10.30, I usually manage to be in bed by eleven. I like to meet up with friends for a drink or to go to the cinema but I need my sleep too.

Grammar
reported statements
▶ CB page 86

1 Look at the answers a candidate gave in a job interview and complete the report the interviewer wrote below.

I studied English and history but I also took modules in French and Italian.

I'm working with an advertising company now and I worked in London before that.

I've been working with the company for two years.

I earn around £24,000.

I really enjoy the teamwork in my current job because I'm a team player.

I prefer to stay where I am at the moment – I don't want to move to London even though it's only an hour to commute on the train and there are regular services.

I am not being stretched in my current job and I need a challenge.

I have good communication skills; I don't have any weaknesses.

I will bring a fresh and different approach to the work – and I'm enthusiastic.

58 | Profile

She said that she **(1)** .... English and history at university but also she **(2)** .... modules in French and Italian. She said currently she **(3)** .... with an advertising company, and **(4)** .... in London before that. She **(5)** .... with her present company for two years. She told me that her current salary was £24,000 and that what she enjoyed about her current job **(6)** .... the teamwork – she explained that she was a team player. When I asked whether she **(7)** .... to London, she replied that she **(8)** .... to stay where she was even though it **(9)** .... only an hour on the train and there **(10)** .... regular services. She said that she wanted the job because she **(11)** .... stretched and that she **(12)** .... a challenge. She said that she had good communication skills, and **(13)** .... any weaknesses and that she **(14)** .... bring a fresh and different approach to her work. She **(15)** .... also enthusiastic. I liked her and would recommend her for the job.

Use of English
Word formation (Part 3)
▶ CB page 87

1 Make the words into nouns or another noun using the suffixes in the box. There is one suffix you do not need to use.

-ant	-ative	-er	-iour	-ism
-ment	-or			

1 tourist
2 application
3 representation
4 improve
5 employment
6 behave

2 For questions 1–8, read the text below. Use the word given in capitals at the end of some of the lines to form a word that fits in the gap in the same line. There is an example at the beginning (0).

What NOT to do at a job interview!

People often feel **(0)** _extremely_ nervous before they go for a job interview and are worried about how to make a good first **(1)** .... on a potential employer. There is lots of advice on the internet about what job **(2)** .... should do to increase their chances of having a **(3)** .... interview, so here are some hot tips on what to avoid. Number one is dress **(4)** .... If you turn up for an office job wearing casual clothes, you will be off to a very bad start. Secondly, avoid too much **(5)** .... – I don't mean with your interviewers who **(6)** .... will expect you to talk to them, but with your friends, who may call you at the most **(7)** .... moment on your mobile phone. Finally, even if you don't get the job, don't take it **(8)** .... Learn from the experience and any mistakes you may have made. Move on to the next opportunity – it will almost certainly be better!

EXTREME

IMPRESS

APPLY
SUCCESS

APPROPRIATE

COMMUNICATE
NATURAL

CONVENIENT

PERSONAL

Writing
Letter of application (Part 2)
▶ CB page 88

About the exam:
In Part 2 of the Writing paper, you may have the opportunity to write a formal letter of application for a job, a course, etc.

Strategy:
- Read the task carefully and underline the key words and phrases.
- Use a formal style and include the following information in this order:
  1 Why you are writing, where you saw the advertisement and which position or course you are applying for.
  2 Why you are a suitable candidate (your skills and qualifications).
  3 When you will be available and how you can be contacted.

1 Look at this task and the letter of application a student wrote. Put the sentences in the correct order.

> You see this advertisement in an international newspaper.
>
> ### Trainee Journalist
> We are looking for an enthusiastic and creative person with a good knowledge of student life and young people's interests to work as a trainee journalist on our most recently launched magazine, *Actualise it!*
>
> We offer flexible working hours and conditions, training on the job and intensive courses in Chinese or English.
>
> Send a letter of application to:
>
> Mark Ellington
> Editor
> *Actualise it!*
> 37 Westwick Gardens
> London
>
> Write your **letter of application** in **140–190** words.

Dear Mr Ellington,

.... I can be contacted by telephone on 01094893214 or by email at SamRuffolo@ymail.com.

.... Also, would it be possible to learn both the languages you mention in your advertisement? I have a good knowledge of English, but can certainly improve and I have always wanted to study Chinese.

.... Firstly, I would like to know whether it would be possible to work from home.

.... I am writing in reply to your advertisement in Tuesday's *Global News*.

.... I would like to ask some questions about the position.

.... I would like to apply for the position of trainee journalist on *Actualise it!* magazine.

Yours sincerely,

2 Now look at these DOs and DON'Ts for job applications and the letter in Activity 1. Tick (✓) the advice the student has followed.

1 ☐ DO say which job you are applying for, and where and when you saw it advertised. Invent a newspaper and date if you need to.

2 ☐ DO mention each of the areas in the advertisement when you write your application.

3 ☐ DO say how you can be contacted.

4 ☐ DON'T forget to mention why you would be suitable.

5 ☐ DO begin and end your letter as you would other formal letters.

3 Read the task in Activity 1 again. Rewrite the student's letter, adding in all the information required. Remember to divide your letter into paragraphs.

Multiple-choice cloze (Part 1)

For questions 1–8, read the text below and decide which answer (A, B, C or D) best fits each gap. There is an example at the beginning (0).

A review of a collection of short stories

This collection of short stories has a wide range of interesting characters. The topics explored are not interrelated as some other collections are – **(0)** _A, instead_ each story covers a different aspect of personal experience.

The first story concerns the psychological **(1)** .... of a decision made by a woman in the heat of the moment. The reader is left to **(2)** .... his or her own mind about whether the woman should feel guilty, though it seemed to me that in this **(3)** .... she shouldn't.

The second story is based on the **(4)** .... of revenge. It follows the victim of a crime, and the way in which she **(5)** .... the situation. Although she may appear to be cruel at times, the reader feels genuine **(6)** .... for her.

Finally, there is an exciting account of what would happen if you **(7)** .... your best friend was leading a secret life as a spy. **(8)** .... it sounds unlikely, the writing is excellent and creates great suspense.

Overall, it's a collection to enjoy and re-read many times.

0	**A** instead	**B** and	**C** despite	**D** though
1	**A** ends	**B** significances	**C** consequences	**D** summaries
2	**A** make over	**B** make out	**C** make up	**D** make for
3	**A** moment	**B** time	**C** place	**D** case
4	**A** movement	**B** argument	**C** sense	**D** theme
5	**A** gets up to	**B** deals with	**C** comes up to	**D** goes with
6	**A** sympathy	**B** identity	**C** sensitivity	**D** consideration
7	**A** found out	**B** looked for	**C** went through	**D** got from
8	**A** Since	**B** Although	**C** In spite of	**D** As

Open cloze (Part 2)

For questions 9–16, read the text below and think of the word which best fits each gap. Use only one word in each gap. There is an example at the beginning (0).

Not ideal – but good enough!

I fell into my first job **(0)** _by_ chance. I'd graduated with a reasonable degree, but I was at **(9)** .... loss to know what to do next. I had no money, but **(10)** .... this I had unrealistic dreams of being able to travel the world. **(11)** .... the end what happened was a happy coincidence. An uncle of mine had set **(12)** .... a language school in the Caribbean, and needed someone to help him run the office. I jumped at the chance, **(13)** .... at the time I had no idea that it would turn out to be a real challenge. There were **(14)** .... many problems to deal with that I couldn't cope, **(15)** .... there were times when I felt overwhelmed. The advantages included good money and fantastic weather, but finally the pressure became too great so I quit. **(16)** .... , working in a school helped me realise that was what I really wanted to do, and now I'm a teacher!

Word formation (Part 3)

For questions 17–24, read the text below. Use the word given in capitals at the end of some of the lines to form a word that fits in the gap in the same line. There is an example at the beginning (0).

The perfect horror novel

What is the most important **(0)** factor in creating a perfect horror novel? The most **(17)** .... horror novelists realise that simply delivering cheap shocks through descriptions of violence is not the best way to do it. **(18)** .... writers appeal to the reader's feelings by creating **(19)** .... characters, and are also able to produce extremely powerful images that stay in the reader's mind **(20)** .... They understand that the most **(21)** .... things are in our own imaginations, not what we actually read on the page.

Of course their novels also work up to a very intense climax, but perfect horror novels involve the reader at an **(22)** .... level and often don't end with any kind of clear **(23)** .... This leaves the reader in a state of suspense. They can suggest that there are many different realities that exist beyond the one we live in, and this creates amazing **(24)** .... for their readers.

	FACT
	SUCCESS
	PROFESSION
	BELIEVE
	DEFINITELY
	SCARE
	EMOTION
	RESOLVE
	POSSIBLE

Key word transformation (Part 4)

For questions 25–30, complete the second sentence so that it has a similar meaning to the first sentence, using the word given. Do not change the word given. You must use between two and five words, including the word given. Here is an example (0).

Example:

0 'Why don't you stay to dinner, Jo?' asked Peter.

INVITED

Peter _invited Jo to stay_ to dinner.

25 'Don't open your present until your birthday,' Carol told Sue.

NOT

Carol told Sue .... until her birthday.

26 'I'm sorry I was late for the meeting,' said Carlo.

APOLOGISED

Carlo .... late for the meeting.

27 I become very upset if I have any pressure at work.

WORKED

I .... if I have any pressure at work.

28 How is your relationship with Mike these days?

GETTING

How .... with Mike these days?

29 You were wrong to tell Jim about the surprise party.

SHOULD

You .... Jim about the surprise party.

30 It rains so much that everyone carries an umbrella.

SUCH

It .... that everyone carries an umbrella.

[To be styled as a business report at next stage]

9 Lucky break?

Reading
Gapped text (Part 6)
▶ CB page 90

1 **You are going to read an article from a psychology magazine. Six sentences have been removed from the text. Read the article and the sentences quickly and choose the best title.**

A Some of us are just born lucky

B There's no such thing as bad luck

C Be lucky – it's an easy skill to learn

2 **Read the article and the sentences again. Choose from the sentences A–G the one which fits each gap. There is one extra sentence which you do not need to use.**

A The same applies to luck.

B Conversely, it's not easy to do this of course.

C I interviewed these people, asked them to complete diaries, questionnaires and intelligence tests, and invited them to participate in experiments.

D Knowing this, I wanted to find out whether people's luck can be enhanced by getting them to think and behave like a lucky person.

E In one interview, a lucky volunteer arrived with his leg in a plaster cast and described how he had fallen down a flight of stairs.

F I designed a series of studies to examine the impact on people's lives of chance opportunities, lucky breaks and being in the right place at the right time.

G On average, the unlucky people took about two minutes to do this, whereas the lucky people took just seconds.

3 **Complete sentences 1–6 with the correct form of the underlined words in the text.**

1 I had a .... you would call round today.

2 Even if you are very fit, you won't finish a marathon without developing more ....

3 His advisors warned him that May was not a good month to .... a new business venture.

4 She does really good work from time to time but she needs to be more ....

5 Her research provided major .... into the causes of the disease.

6 My friend finds his work as a psychologist extremely ....

A decade ago, I set out to investigate luck. [1] After many experiments, I believe that I now understand why some people are luckier than others and that it is possible to become luckier.

To <u>launch</u> my study, I placed advertisements in national newspapers, asking for people who felt lucky or unlucky to contact me. Over the years, 400 extraordinary men and women from all walks of life volunteered for my research. [2] The findings revealed that although unlucky people have very little <u>insight</u> into the causes of their good and bad luck, their thoughts and behaviour are to blame.

Take chance opportunities. Lucky people <u>consistently</u> encounter such opportunities, whereas unlucky people do not. I carried out a simple experiment to find out why this was so. I gave both lucky and unlucky people a newspaper, and asked them to look through it and tell me how many photographs were inside. [3] Why? Because the second page of the newspaper contained the message: 'There are 43 photographs in this newspaper.' This message took up half a page and was written in large type but the unlucky people tended to miss it.

Unlucky people are generally far more anxious than lucky people. We know that anxiety disrupts people's ability to notice the unexpected. In another experiment, people were asked to watch a moving dot in the centre of a computer screen. Without warning, large dots would occasionally appear at the edges of the screen. Nearly all participants noticed these. The experiment was then repeated with a second group of people, who were offered a financial <u>reward</u> for accurately watching the centre dot. Offering money like this creates anxiety. People tried to focus on the centre dot and tended not to notice the large dots appearing at the sides of the screen. The harder they looked, the less they saw. [4] Unlucky people miss chance opportunities because they are too focused on looking for something else.

Lucky people use four basic principles to generate good fortune: they create and notice opportunities, they listen to their intuition, they have positive expectations, and they are able to see the positive side of bad luck. [5] I designed exercises to help the volunteers spot chance opportunities, listen to their intuition, expect to be lucky, and be more <u>resilient</u> to bad luck. After a month of doing the exercises, the results were dramatic: The unlucky people became lucky and the lucky people became luckier.

My studies show that unlucky people can learn to take advantage of opportunities, to trust their <u>hunches</u>, expect things to turn out well and even to see the positive side of ill fortune just as lucky people do. [6] I asked him whether he still felt lucky and he cheerfully explained that he felt luckier than before. As he pointed out, he could have broken his neck.

Vocabulary

chance, opportunity and *possibility*
► CB page 91

1 Use the words in the box to complete these sentences. You will need to use some words more than once.

a	any	at	by	earliest	good
in	leave	slight	take	the	
to	with				

1 Don't just .... things .... chance. It's better to plan.

2 Look at those black clouds. There's .... chance it will rain later.

3 We decided to .... chance and try that new restaurant opposite the park.

4 The interview went well and I think I might be .... chance for the job.

5 Would you happen to know the way to the museum .... chance?

6 I ran into my old friend Kirsti completely .... chance the other day.

7 .... opportunity, I hope to go abroad for a few years.

8 There's .... possibility that I might be in Madrid in June.

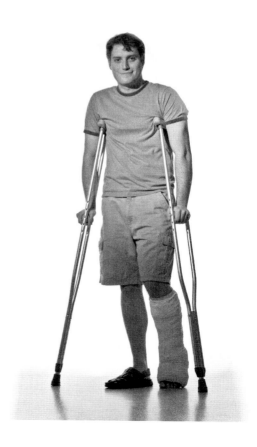

Grammar
conditional forms
▶ CB page 92

1 Match 1–6 to endings A–I to make sentences. There are some endings that you do not need to use.

1 If I play tennis with you on Saturday afternoon,
2 If I spend too much money every month,
3 If I moved to live in another country,
4 If I drink too much coffee,
5 If I go to the disco on Saturday night,
6 If I walked under a ladder,

A I find it difficult to sleep.
B I would have a lot of bad luck.
C I am not able to pay my credit card bill.
D I will get a job more easily.
E I would be able to go out with my friends.
F I would miss my family a lot.
G I will probably meet a lot of my friends there.
H I can't have a good time.
I I will not have time to go out in the evening.

2 For questions 1–6, complete the second sentence so that it has a similar meaning to the first sentence, using the word given. Do not change the word given. You must use between two and five words, including the word given.

1 You can't smoke in restaurants without getting into trouble.
   SMOKE
   If you .... get into trouble.

2 The only thing stopping me doing my homework is that I don't have my dictionary here.
   IF
   I .... I had my dictionary here.

3 You'll get wet because it's probably going to rain.
   IT
   If .... get wet.

4 I am not very good at typing but it would be useful for my job if I could do it.
   WERE
   It would be useful for my job if .... at typing.

5 People often find it difficult to concentrate in noisy places.
   THEY
   When .... people often find it difficult to concentrate.

6 I refused to swim when the sea was rough.
   NOT
   If the sea was rough, I .... swimming.

Use of English
Word formation (Part 3)
▶ CB page 93

1 Complete the sentences with the correct form of the word *compete*.

1 Sandra is a fantastic .... She never gives up.
2 He won an underwater photography .... The prize was a scuba-diving holiday in Thailand.
3 Denise says that she isn't a .... person but she hates to lose.
4 Those new exercise machines are quite .... priced. I think I might get one.

2 For questions 1–8, read the text below. Use the word given in capitals at the end of some of the lines to form a word that fits in the gap in the same line.

Do we make our own luck?

We all rely on an element of luck to get by, but where does it come from and why do some people appear to be **(0)** consistently lucky or unlucky? **CONSISTENT**
Richard has spent years investigating this and says it's not **(1)** .... or psychic **INTELLIGENT**
ability that matters but a person's approach to life. He has some advice for people seeking an **(2)** .... in their luck. **IMPROVE**

'If you expect to be **(3)** .... , then sadly **FORTUNE**
you often will be. Accept that bad luck will happen but turn it around by imagining how things could have been worse and looking for **(4)** .... to a **SOLVE**
problem.'

So the secret is learning to look at life **(5)** .... Richard now runs courses, **DIFFERENT**
helping people to change their mindset. Trish says that before attending the course she was prone to **(6)** .... in her **HAPPY**
personal life. Now she has a more positive outlook. Since changing her **(7)** .... , by not looking for bad luck, **BEHAVE**
she feels luckier.

So those **(8)** .... people who keep **ANNOY**
telling us to cheer up and look on the bright side may be right after all!

Listening
Multiple choice (Part 4)
▶ CB page 94

1 ▶ 18 **You will hear a radio interview with Carol Johnson, a successful young racing cyclist. For questions 1–7, choose the best answer (A, B or C).**

1 Why did Carol start cycling?

   A Her parents encouraged her.

   B A younger person made her jealous.

   C She wanted to do something better than her friend.

2 How does Carol describe herself?

   A overly competitive in all situations

   B too introverted to mix with others

   C sensible in her approach to sport

3 According to Carol, her training programme is

   A important for developing a routine.

   B crucial for developing the best technique.

   C necessary for developing the right mental attitude.

4 What does Carol say about sportspeople in general?

   A They're less confident than they appear.

   B They're extremely self-centred.

   C They're often worried about getting injured.

5 What is Carol's attitude to luck?

   A It's more important than anything else.

   B It's balanced by practical techniques.

   C It's limited to certain types of racing.

6 How does Carol feel about the media attention?

   A It has become an unnecessary part of her sport.

   B It's difficult to deal with sometimes.

   C It stops her getting financial support.

7 What advice does Carol have for young cyclists?

   A Plan for life after sport.

   B Keep things in perspective.

   C Enjoy success while it lasts.

2 **Match 1–6 to A–F to make collocations.**

1 ride   **A** about an achievement

2 boast   **B** a goal

3 take up **C** a bike

4 keep   **D** your best

5 achieve **E** your mouth shut

6 do   **F** a new sport

Grammar
third conditional
▶ CB page 95

1 **Complete the sentences with the correct form of the words in the box.**

buy	go out	give	know
make	meet	see	win

1 You .... the match easily if you had practised more.

2 If I .... how much fun surfing is, I'd have started doing it years ago.

3 If I'd realised the film was on television last night, I ....

4 If I hadn't gone on holiday to France last year, I .... Sue.

5 If I .... more money when I was younger, I would have been able to buy a house by now.

6 I .... Mike at the party if I had arrived earlier but I'm not sure whether he was there.

7 I .... the car if it had been cheaper, though I'm not sure.

2 **For questions 1–6, complete the second sentence so that it has a similar meaning to the first sentence, using the word given. Do not change the word given.**

1 Given more time, I'd have been able to finish all the work.

   HAD

   If I .... , I'd have been able to finish all the work.

2 Jo would have been very upset if he hadn't had an invitation to our party.

   NOT

   If we .... to the party, Jo would have been very upset.

3 George turned up late for the meeting because his alarm didn't go off.

   IF

   George would not have been late for the meeting .... off.

4 It's very unfortunate that the referee didn't give a penalty as the team would have won the game.

   LOST

   It's very unfortunate; if the referee had given a penalty, the team .... the game.

5 It's lucky that I have got a car otherwise I'd have to use the bus.

   GOT

   If .... a car, I'd have to use the bus.

6 I didn't have the right tools to finish the job, so I had to leave it.

   HAD

   If I'd had the right tools to finish the job, I .... leave it.

Speaking
Discussion (Part 4)
▶ CB page 96

1 Look at compensation strategies 1 and 2. Would you use them to a) give you time to think or b) stop the other candidate from interrupting you?

1 Well, it's difficult to say … **2** OK, let me see …

2 ▶ 19 **Two students are discussing some questions in Paper 4, Part 4. Listen and complete their conversation.**

I = Interlocutor, D = David, S = Sara

I: Do you think luck is important in life?

D: (1) .... Well, I always wish my friends good luck before an exam or job interview so I suppose that does mean I believe in it to some extent. What about you?

S: Me too – and I really believe it makes a difference. I always carry a – I'm not sure how to say this in English – it's <u>a little thing that is supposed to be lucky</u>. It's a silver bead that my grandmother gave me. If I did an exam without it, I know I would fail.

D: (2) .... that you actually think it affects your success in the exam?

S: Well, yes. I do.

D: Well, I suppose I do too now I come to think of it. I have things I always do like wearing the same socks and walking on the same side of the street on the way to the exam.

I: How much does luck contribute to success in sporting events?

D: (3) .... but not so much, in my opinion. **(4)** .... other things are more important like – I can't remember the word – <u>how well you can do things</u> like hit the ball or passing in football.

S: But in tennis, for example, you often see that for one player the ball hits the top of the – what's it called? – you know, <u>the long thing that divides the court into two halves</u> – and the ball doesn't go over. That's to do with luck if you ask me.

D: So you think luck is more important?

S: No, not always. **(5)** .... that in some sports it can play quite an important role. I'm very superstitious. There are a lot of things that I avoid doing, like stepping on the lines on the pavement or walking under <u>those things that you use to climb up to paint the house</u> – and if I do, my English friends tell me to say 'bread and butter'!

D: Why?

S: (6) ...., it's supposed to stop anything terrible happening to you.

D: But perhaps some superstitions are logical.

S: What do you mean?

D: (7) .... that sometimes there really is a danger. For example, the painter could drop something and it could fall on you and cause some kind of <u>harm or damage to you physically</u>.

I: Do superstitions ever stop people doing things they might enjoy or benefit from?

D: (8) .... enjoy?

I: Yes.

D: (9) .... I suppose they do but I would never decide not to go on a trip or something because it was on the thirteenth of the month.

S: (10) .... that if you go to the airport and the airline gave you seat 13D on the plane, you would still go?

D: Well, I might feel a bit … <u>not exactly afraid but kind of a bit worried and uncomfortable</u> but it wouldn't stop me flying.

3 Match the underlined paraphrases the students used in Activity 2 to words 1–6.

1 ladders   **3** uneasy   **5** good luck charm
2 skill   **4** injury   **6** net

Vocabulary
collocations: success and failure
▶ CB page 97

1 Cross out the word or phrase in italics that does <u>not</u> collocate with the verbs in bold.

1 **have** *a bad day/a lucky break/a brilliant sporting career/an enormous effort*

2 **fulfil** *a lifelong ambition/ her early potential/an important obligation/a good deed*

3 **set** *a strong demand/a reasonable target/a high standard/a clear limit*

4 **make** *a go of something/a good try/a favourable impression/a serious attempt*

5 **overcome** *considerable obstacles/anxiety/a sporting competition/a difficult past*

2 Choose the correct option in italics to complete the sentences.

1 In sport it's vital to know how to cope *with/for/to* success as well as failure.

2 She just couldn't face *out/up/on* to the fact that her sporting career was over.

3 He's taken *in/on/after* some new challenges and has really improved his game.

4 She decided to focus *at/in/on* improving her serve and backhand.

5 Our national team are going *for/at/to* three gold medals in the athletics at the next Olympics.

6 He was so exhausted he gave *in/on/over* to an overwhelming urge to stop and rest.

Writing
Essay (Part 1)
▶ CB page 98

1 Look at the task below and read the plans (A and B). Which plan matches the essay the student actually wrote?

In your English class you have been talking about how luck influences success in sport. Now, your English teacher has asked you to write an essay.

In many sports, luck is sometimes more important than skill or physical fitness. Do you agree with this?

Notes
Write about:
1 luck
2 skill
3 .... (your own idea)

A

Introduction: repeat the statement in the title in different words

Paragraph 2: luck is more important (example)

Paragraph 3: skill is more important (example)

Paragraph 4: motivation plays an equal part (example)

Conclusion: summarise main points and give my opinion

B

Introduction: say whether I agree or disagree with the statement in my own words

Paragraph 2: arguments to support my point of view with examples

Paragraph 3: arguments to support the opposite point of view with examples

Paragraph 4: arguments to assess point of view with examples

Conclusion: sum up and repeat my point of view in different words

(1) It is often said that luck is the most important factor in sporting success and it has more influence than physical fitness and skill.

There are aspects of sport where luck plays a part. Let's take a penalty kick in football **(2)** as an example. A goalkeeper who moves in the same direction as the ball and stops it going into the goal has probably just been lucky rather than skilful.

(3) It is clear, **(4)** on the other hand, that skill and fitness contribute most to success in many other circumstances. **(5)** This is true of tennis, for example. If a ball hits the net, is it because a player is unlucky? The player himself would probably say he had made a mistake and his skill was not good enough.

The last factor in success is motivation; a runner who is really determined to win trains harder and then tries harder than other competitors, and so wins races.

(6) To sum up, although luck does occasionally influence the outcome in some sports, **(7)** in my opinion there is simply no substitute for skill, fitness and determination.

2 Choose phrases from the box to substitute the underlined sections of the essay. There is one extra phrase you do not need.

as an illustration of this point   in conclusion
in contrast   it is my view that   nevertheless
many people claim that   this can be said of
we can easily see

3 Put the instructions for planning and writing an essay A–E into the correct order.

A Check carefully for mistakes with spelling and grammar, especially verbs and conditionals.

B Choose one of the plans from Activity 1 (they are both good plans).

C Write your essay.

D Make notes of ideas and reasons for the ideas in the task.

E Think of your own ideas.

4 Read the task below and write your answer. Use 140–190 words.

In your English class you have been talking about sport in school. Now, your English teacher has asked you to write an essay.

Not all schools have sport as a compulsory subject. Do you think this is a good thing?

Notes
Write about:
1 health
2 new interests
3 .... (your own idea)

10 Friends for life

Vocabulary
compound adjectives: personality ▶ CB page 103

1 Cross out the adjective in each list which cannot form a compound adjective with the word in bold.

1 even/hot/cross/quick **-tempered**

2 empty/hard/level/heavy **-headed**

3 mild/well/friendly/ill **-mannered**

4 warm/hot/cold/kind **-hearted**

5 strong/weak/quick/ill **-willed**

6 single/open/like/fixed **-minded**

Listening
Multiple matching (Part 3) ▶ CB page 103

1 ▶ 20 **You will hear five people talking about friendship. For questions 1–5, choose from the list (A–H) what each speaker says is most important to them in a friendship. Use each letter only once. There are three extra letters which you do not need to use.**

A frequent contact

B mutual trust

C shared interests

D absolute honesty

E emotional support

F similar personalities

G a sense of humour

H same experience of school

Speaker 1 ☐

Speaker 2 ☐

Speaker 3 ☐

Speaker 4 ☐

Speaker 5 ☐

Grammar
conditional linking words ▶ CB page 104

1 Choose the correct options in italics to complete the sentences.

1 It's very easy for friends to keep in contact *unless/as long as* they use Facebook or Twitter.

2 I always try to phone my friend every evening *unless/whether* I know she's out.

3 It's good to keep in touch with friends *otherwise/even if* it can be a hassle sometimes.

4 Whenever I travel I keep in touch via Facebook *whether/otherwise* my friends miss me.

5 I take an umbrella with me when I go out, *even if/whether* it's not raining.

6 It's a good idea to make plans, *otherwise/unless* things can go wrong.

7 My friend always comes shopping with me *whether/even if* I don't want her to.

8 You'll pass the exam *unless/provided that* you work hard.

9 You can borrow my laptop *as long as/even if* you promise to take care of it.

10 I don't know *whether/as long as* it's a good idea to call him.

11 I'll call you tonight *unless/otherwise* I hear from you first.

2 Complete sentences 1–5 with the correct form of the verbs in the box.

| argue | buy | cook | learn | stand |

1 You won't be able to live in Italy unless you .... speak Italian.

2 Even if you .... your new television on the internet, you wouldn't have got a better deal.

3 I'll help you with your work this evening as long as you .... the meal.

4 He'll give you a lift to work provided that you .... at the corner of the street at 8a.m.

5 We never talk about politics, otherwise we .... all the time.

3 For questions 1–6, complete the second sentence so that it has a similar meaning to the first sentence, using the word given. Do not change the word given. You must use between two and five words, including the word given.

1 Without using a dictionary, I'm sure I won't understand the article.

   UNLESS

   I'm sure I won't understand the article .... a dictionary.

2 I won't help you unless you agree to come out tomorrow.

   LONG

   I will only .... you agree to come out tomorrow.

3 I clean my teeth every night so that they won't decay.

   OTHERWISE

   I clean my teeth every night .... decay.

4 I'll finish the report if they give me enough time to do it.

   THAT

   I'll finish the report .... enough time to do it.

5 I found the job rather boring but at least the salary was good.

   EVEN

   The salary was good .... was rather boring.

6 Have you decided to invite Joe to the party?

   WHETHER

   Have you decided .... Joe to the party?

Use of English
Multiple-choice cloze (Part 1)
▶ CB page 105

1 Choose the correct options in italics to complete the sentences.

1 That painting is *particular/unique*. It's one of a kind.

2 I'm worried about Harry – he's not as cheerful as *typical/usual*.

3 It's easier to learn if you get *individual/unique* attention.

4 I like keeping up with *current/present* affairs so I watch the news on TV.

5 Surprisingly, it's quite *common/actual* for people to argue with close friends.

6 I'm sorry, I don't know the *actual/present* truth about the affair.

2 For questions 1–8, read the text below and decide which word (A, B, C or D) best fits each gap. There is an example at the beginning (0).

To tweet or not to tweet?

Some people claim social networking sites have a negative impact on people's ability to make friends in **(0)** D, real life. There has been a **(1)** .... deal of speculation about the long-term impact of their use on people's social lives and much of it has **(2)** .... on the possibility that these sites are **(3)** .... users' relationships, pushing them away from participating in the offline world. Twitter 'friends' may become more important than neighbours. However, **(4)** .... to such fears, recent research suggests that people who use such sites actually have a higher **(5)** .... of close relationships and are more **(6)** .... to be involved in civic and political activities than those who don't. Social networking sites help people with busy lives find ways of **(7)** .... in touch and providing regular updates. The world of networked individuals will certainly **(8)** .... evolving, so who knows what the future holds for our personal relationships?

0	**A** actual	**B** true	**C** right	**D** real
1	**A** big	**B** great	**C** huge	**D** large
2	**A** centred	**B** looked	**C** examined	**D** investigated
3	**A** cutting	**B** wounding	**C** injuring	**D** damaging
4	**A** opposing	**B** contrary	**C** opposite	**D** contrasting
5	**A** collection	**B** amount	**C** number	**D** group
6	**A** likely	**B** probable	**C** possible	**D** expected
7	**A** holding	**B** staying	**C** continuing	**D** maintaining
8	**A** turn up	**B** get through	**C** carry on	**D** make out

Reading
Multiple choice (Part 5)
▶ CB page 106

1 **You are going to read an article giving advice about how to end a friendship. Read the article once quickly and say which of the points 1–4 below are not mentioned.**

1 breaking up with someone you've been going out with

2 'unfriending' someone on a social networking site

3 having an argument with an old friend

4 how women regard friendship

2 **Read the article again. For questions 1–6, choose the answer (A, B, C or D) which you think fits best according to the text.**

1 Why, according to the author, is it sometimes easier to end a romantic relationship?

  A Your friends comfort you more.

  B You can blame your ex-partner for what happened.

  C You can get specialised advice about what to do.

  D You and your partner understand that a change has taken place.

2 What can go wrong with the 'slow fade out' approach?

  A You may lose all the friends you have in common.

  B You might keep running into the friend you want to lose.

  C Your friend might not notice what you are doing.

  D Your friend might realise you actually want to end the friendship.

3 How, according to Jodyne L. Speyer, should you tell your friend that it's over?

  A You should be unkind if necessary.

  B You should say you never want to see them again.

  C You should give them as many reasons as possible for ending the friendship.

  D You should briefly explain why you want to end the friendship.

4 Why do people often feel they have failed when a friendship ends?

  A The process has taken too long.

  B Others admire us less if we lose our friends.

  C It's natural to think that friendships last for ever.

  D They have false expectations of friendship.

5 What does the word 'they' in line 57 refer to?

  A friends

  B things

  C friendships

  D women

6 How does the author feel about the break-up of friendships?

  A accepting of the fact that they happen

  B cynical about the way they often end

  C critical of people who end them

  D optimistic about relationships in general

3 **Match the underlined words in the article with meanings 1–6.**

1 make less intense

2 rejected

3 communicate

4 becomes less close

5 opposite

6 pointlessly continue

4 **Complete the sentences with the correct form of the underlined words in the article.**

1 The boat broke loose from its mooring and .... out to sea.

2 The fruit juice was very sweet so we .... it with water.

3 They were fined for .... their old fridge in the street.

4 He put the car into .... and backed into the parking space.

5 I'm always accidentally .... on my cat's tail.

6 Wait till the soup .... a bit. It's too hot to eat.

Vocabulary
phrasal verbs with *come*
▶ CB page 107

1 **Use the prepositions in the box to complete the sentences. You can use some of them more than once.**

| across | into | out | round to |
| through | up | up with | round |

1 I was really surprised when the exam results came .... I did much better than I'd expected.

2 My parents didn't like the idea of my going away for a gap year at first but eventually they came .... it.

3 Charlie came .... a fortune when a distant aunt of his in Australia died.

How to lose friends

I should have seen it coming. There was no big betrayal, no rows about money but the spark had gone. The end, when it came, was swift: 'We may as well call it a day,' I was told. In shock, I called my sister and told her the news. 'Oh no, you've been <u>dumped</u>,' she said. And indeed I had, but not by a boyfriend. By a friend.

When a romantic relationship ends, things are relatively simple. There are broken hearts, recriminations. Mutual friends choose sides. No matter how upsetting, at least it's clear: you were a couple and now you're not. When a friendship <u>cools</u>, it's seldom so straightforward. The experts, however, are on hand to offer help. As far as they're concerned there are two possible ways to end it.

First we have what I call 'the slow fade out'. Irene Levine, Professor of Psychiatry at New York University and author of a book on the subject explains: 'Sometimes it's possible to downgrade the relationship by seeing the person less or to <u>dilute</u> it by seeing the person with a group.' If you have a lot of mutual friends, or are likely still to see each other, 'downgrading' makes things less awkward, but if the friend is too naive or self-absorbed to read the signals, or just really persistent, it may not be enough. Eventually you may need to do the decent thing and dump them properly.

It's then that you need the other method where you actually tell the person that the friendship is over, and that takes courage and honesty. It doesn't have to be cruel but it does mean telling someone you were once close to why you feel they are no longer worthy of your time. No one likes to hear that, so you need to <u>tread</u> carefully, warns Jodyne L. Speyer, author of another book on dealing with this problem.

Speyer suggests giving a warning: 'If you tell me something's wrong, maybe I can fix it, and if I can't, then at least I knew this was coming, so it prepares me. And be kind about it, say "Here's what's not working." I don't need 100 reasons, but let me know what the problem is, so I can have that information and move on. I don't have to agree with it but at least I have something.' This is difficult to do, of course, but according to Speyer it gets easier with practice:

'When you're clear about your feelings, other people respond to that. You may think you're doing someone a favour by not telling them you don't want to continue with the friendship but in the long run it can make it worse.'

Even so, however gently you break the news, chances are someone will feel hurt and resist. 'Most friendships, even very good ones, don't last for ever,' Levine says. 'Yet women particularly are brought up to believe the romanticised notion of "best friends forever". In our culture, we are judged by our ability to make and keep friends, so we have a hard time getting over the loss of a best friend and see it as a personal failure.' Things are made worse by the fact that many end so slowly. 'When friendships <u>drift</u>, we rarely discuss it,' says relationship psychotherapist Paula Hall. 'Because they usually don't end in conflict, there is no closure. You don't feel you're better off without each other, it just stops, so there can be feelings of loss.'   line 57

Joseph Epstein, another friendship expert, compares today's friendships to the seating in a sports stadium: your closest friends sit with you in the box seats, secondary friends are in the grandstand seats and the rest are in the stands. But, according to Epstein, there is hope, even in the cheap seats, because friendships aren't static, so people can move from one area of the stadium to another. Someone who starts out in the stands – perhaps a classmate or neighbour – can be promoted via the grandstand to the box seats. Sadly, the <u>reverse</u> is also true and that's when we need to know how to end it all.

4 Coming .... that old photo of Hugh when I was tidying the house made me feel a bit sad.

5 You should smile a bit more. You sometimes come .... as being a bit unfriendly.

6 Peter's birthday is coming .... next month, so we should start to make some plans for a party.

7 I don't know who came .... the design for the new building but I think it looks very strange.

8 My grandparents suffered a lot when they were young but somehow they managed to come .... it all.

9 It took me ages to persuade him, but now he's coming .... to my way of thinking.

10 When the news came .... about his promotion, everyone was so pleased.

2 Replace the underlined words in the sentences with a phrasal verb with *come* in the correct form.

1 I was thrilled when I heard I'd <u>inherited</u> some money from a long-lost uncle in Australia.

2 it's easy to <u>find</u> interesting things <u>by chance</u> when you're surfing the internet.

3 I hated the idea of taking an extra maths course, but I <u>survived</u> it and it was useful.

4 The tennis season is <u>starting</u> next week, so I'm planning which tournaments to enter.

5 I find it easy to <u>think of</u> new ideas to write about.

6 My mother wasn't keen on the idea of my becoming a musician, but now she's <u>accepted</u> it.

7 I know people think I'm strong-willed because I <u>look</u> as if I'm confident, but that's just an act!

8 I think the new timetable is <u>going to be released</u> at 12.00 today.

Grammar
participles (*-ing* and *-ed*)
▶ CB page 108

1 Change the participle clauses into relative clauses in sentences 1–8 below.

0 There is a shop selling bread near my house.
   There is a shop which sells bread near my house.

1 There was a steel box in the cupboard containing lots of old photographs.

2 That new shop opening in the High Street on Saturday looks like it'll be really good.

3 There is a path leading down to the sea from our hotel.

4 She found the camera belonging to my sister.

5 All those wishing to buy a ticket should queue up near the box office.

6 My best friend is a lively person bursting with energy.

7 I'd love to get a job in film involving set design.

8 My friend gave me a beautiful photograph taken by her brother.

2 Find and correct the mistakes in sentences 1–10 below.

1 I remember meet my friend for the first time – I didn't like him at first!

2 He introduced himself by say 'Howdie!'

3 Once we became friends we didn't stop to talk.

4 We were both interesting in playing football.

5 People said we would end up play professionally together, though sadly that didn't happen.

6 When he moved to another town I missed to speak to him every day.

7 After have been so close, it was hard at first.

8 Now we share our experiences on Facebook and that's fascinated.

9 He's good at take photographs, so I like looking at them on the computer.

10 I hope that we'll carry on be friends forever.

Speaking
Collaborative task (Part 3)
▶ CB page 109

spending time together

being the same age

Are these things really necessary in a good friendship?

liking the same things

living near each other

being trustworthy

1 ▶ 21 Look at the task and listen to the examiner's instructions to the two candidates. Decide if this statement is true (T) or false (F).

Each candidate is supposed to choose the most important prompt.

2 Now decide which one is <u>not</u> important in a good friendship.

3 Look at some of the things that candidates said in response to the instructions and match them with items 1–5.

A What I mean is, trust is crucial.

B I've always said that friends need an interest in common. Would you agree with that?

C Well, that's certainly true in my case.

D Sorry. I interrupted you. What were you saying?

E No, I suppose not but what if you were a vegetarian and your friends kept inviting you to barbecues?

1 encouraging the other person to say something

2 asking the other candidate to repeat what he/she said

3 showing that you share the other candidate's opinion

4 raising an objection to what the other candidate has said

5 explaining something

4 **Use the words in the box to complete these ways of saying that things are important or unimportant in choosing friends. You need to use some of the words more than once.**

| factors | influence | matters | vital |

1 I don't think having the same musical tastes .... much.

2 Going to the same school or college has a big .... on who you end up being friends with.

3 Knowing that my friends have the same values really .... to me.

4 In my opinion liking the same foods really isn't all that ....

5 For me it's really .... that the person likes animals as much as I do.

6 Sharing a hobby or interest is probably one of the most significant ....

Writing
Article (Part 2)
▶ CB page 110

1 **Look at the task below and the points a student noted down to include in his/her article. Cross out the points that are not relevant.**

You see this advertisement on an English language website.

Articles wanted

A great place for meeting friends!

Where do you meet them? Why is it such a good place? How could it be improved?

Write us an article in 140–190 words answering these questions. We will publish the best articles on our website.

1 reasons young people have a lot of friends
2 what parents think about the place
3 how people get there
4 the need for parking
5 what we do there
6 what makes the place special
7 a description of my friends
8 other places to meet friends

2 **Look at the opening paragraphs (A and B) of two different answers to the task in Activity 1. Which one is more interesting?**

A   Where I meet my friends
It's important to meet friends. My friends like getting together at the weekend so we meet either on Friday night or Saturday morning. One nice place is the café in the town centre, which has tables and chairs outside and cheap cakes. We have a nice time talking.

B   A fantastic place to meet
It's great if there is a place where young people can meet to relax, chat and have a good time. There's an amazing café in my town, which has live music; not only can we hang out there, but there's a really fun atmosphere as well.

3 **Now read the main part of the article. Replace the underlined words with more interesting adjectives from the box.**

| challenging | convenient | exciting |
| interesting | live | quiet |

It's a really **(1)** nice .... place in the evenings because it is busy. There is always something happening and you can even dance to the **(2)** nice .... music. Sometimes there are **(3)** nice .... games or quizzes, which are fun to do with friends and you learn something, even if they're hard! It's **(4)** nice .... to meet new people, too, although if the music is loud, it can be difficult to talk to them because you can't hear what they're saying. It would be much better if there were a **(5)** nice .... room somewhere so that people can just talk to each other there. It would also be **(6)** nice .... if the space at the back could have a bike rack so that we can leave our bikes there. That would be much better because at the moment we have to leave them outside on the pavement.

4 **Choose the best ending for the article.**

A To sum up, this is a very good place to meet friends.

B All in all, just imagine what a great time you'd have if you were able to come and join us!

C It's the coolest place I know.

5 **Now write your own answer to the task in Activity 1.**

Multiple-choice cloze (Part 1)

For questions 1–8, read the text below and decide which answer (A, B, C or D) best fits each gap. There is an example at the beginning (0).

Can we have a close relationship with dolphins?

We've long suspected that there is some kind of **(0)** <u>A. empathy</u> between dolphins and humans – but is there any **(1)** .... of meaningful two-way communication with them? A group of scientists are trying to establish an interactive connection with them by 'co-creating' a language with dolphins that humans can **(2)** .... Captive dolphins can already be **(3)** .... to understand hundreds of words, and can **(4)** .... understand simple grammar. However, until now people could neither understand nor **(5)** .... to the underwater noises dolphins use to communicate with each other.

Now scientists have **(6)** .... a small device comprising a computer and two hydrophones which are **(7)** .... of detecting the full range of dolphin sounds.

But will we really be able to understand them? The image we all have of dolphins is that they are kind-hearted and friendly – what if it **(8)** .... that they're not looking for our friendship at all? That in fact they are really cold-hearted? That would be a real disappointment!

0	**A** empathy	**B** sense	**C** comfort	**D** support
1	**A** luck	**B** chance	**C** destiny	**D** fate
2	**A** solve	**B** see	**C** hear	**D** interpret
3	**A** trained	**B** exercised	**C** practised	**D** rehearsed
4	**A** yet	**B** still	**C** even	**D** however
5	**A** respond	**B** answer	**C** return	**D** acknowledge
6	**A** carried out	**B** taken off	**C** come up with	**D** got down to
7	**A** suited	**B** capable	**C** competent	**D** able
8	**A** gives up	**B** comes across	**C** goes on	**D** turns out

Open cloze (Part 2)

For questions 9–16, read the text below and think of the word which best fits each gap. Use only one word in each gap. There is an example at the beginning (0).

Why do they do it?

Everybody knows that nothing comes easily **(0)** <u>in</u> sport. Success is made **(9)** .... of a combination of hard work and practice, with **(10)** .... little bit of luck thrown in. So how does anyone achieve **(11)** .... right balance? Clearly genetics plays a part – the type of body anyone is born with may come down to chance, and certainly some athletes tend to be more prone to injury, **(12)** .... is unlucky for them. But nothing can beat the hours of training and sheer effort that goes into creating a complete sportsperson. **(13)** .... successful athletes need is to want that success more than anything **(14)** .... That kind of motivation can't be taught, it **(15)** .... to come from inside themselves. It's a deep desire that forces them to go on, **(16)** .... difficult it might seem at times. When you think how many of us find it hard to even go to the gym regularly, that kind of determination has to be admired!

Word formation (Part 3)

For questions 17–24, read the text below. Use the word given in capitals at the end of some of the lines to form a word that fits in the gap in the same line. There is an example at the beginning (0).

What is a friend?

I'm sure we all think we're **(0)** _supportive_ when friends need help, but are we fooling ourselves? To understand the true nature of **(17)** .... , we need to look at our attitude towards those we consider friends, and assess our **(18)** .... towards them.

SUPPORT

FRIEND

BEHAVE

Some people think being a good friend means being a good **(19)** .... While there is some truth in this, it's **(20)** .... if you sit quietly and don't offer advice when it's needed. Of course you shouldn't be too forceful in the **(21)** .... you provide, but making a gentle suggestion should fit the bill. It's important to be **(22)** .... as well as practical.

LISTEN
POINT

ASSIST

SYMPATHY

When a friend is constantly complaining or creating a general atmosphere of **(23)** .... it can be hard to tolerate their moods. It's easier to turn our backs on them and walk away. But that's when **(24)** .... should kick in, and that means sticking with your friend through bad times as well as good.

HAPPY

LOYAL

It would be nice if we could live up to these criteria!

Key word transformation (Part 4)

For questions 25–30, complete the second sentence so that it has a similar meaning to the first sentence, using the word given. Do not change the word given. You must use between two and five words, including the word given. Here is an example (0).

Example:

0   I don't mind going to a party on my own if I know other people who will be there.

PROVIDED

I don't mind going to a party on my own _provided that there will be_ other people there who I know.

25   In the event of heavy snow, we will cancel the game.

IT

If .... , we will cancel the game.

26   If you don't do any practice, you won't get any better.

UNLESS

You won't get any better .... practice.

27   We should get to the airport on time if there isn't any heavy traffic on the motorway.

AS

We should get to the airport in time .... no heavy traffic on the motorway.

28   You missed the plane because you didn't check in on time.

CAUGHT

If you had checked in on time, ... the plane.

29   I want to go to Australia but I don't have enough money.

HAD

If I .... go to Australia.

30   The man living next door always sings loudly every morning.

WHO

The man .... always sings loudly every morning.

Vocabulary
risk and adventure

1 Match 1–8 with A–H to make collocations related to risk and adventure.

1	lone	**A**	clothing
2	risk	**B**	yachtswoman
3	roller	**C**	boarding
4	snow	**D**	diving
5	safety	**E**	coaster
6	sky	**F**	helmet
7	protective	**G**	driving
8	reckless	**H**	taker

Reading
Gapped text (Part 6)
▶ CB page 112

1 You are going to read an article about someone who is trying to do something outside his comfort zone. Six sentences have been removed from the article. Read the article and decide if statements 1–3 are true (T) or false (F).

1 It is the mental challenge that motivates Johnny.
2 Johnny is worried that he might not be strong enough.
3 Johnny is only doing this because he wants to become famous.

2 Read the article and the sentences again. Choose from the sentences A–G the one that best fits each gap (1–6). There is one extra sentence which you do not need to use.

A Then last autumn, out of the blue and without telling his friends where he was going or what he was planning, he cancelled all his engagements.

B Naturally, this is something that involves a lot of repetition.

C However, in spite of what could be a potential problem, Johnny isn't bothered about it at all.

D He is, though, somewhat fitter as a result of all his endeavours.

E If he makes it back by early afternoon, he turns round and does it all over again.

F It's an odd admission for someone who has spent the past six months running up and down the Welsh mountains every day, and even stranger when you know why.

G He was thrilled when they invited him to take their physical fitness tests.

A SHORT HOP TO PARIS

Johnny Budden claims that he hates running. 'It's so boring,' he complains. [1] Beginning on 1 April, Budden plans to run from John O'Groats to Paris – a total of 1,000 miles – in a month, averaging more than a marathon every day.

Surprisingly, Budden has no background in <u>endurance</u> sports. Going by the name 'Sticky', he is one of the world's foremost practitioners of parkour, also known as 'freerunning'. It's a sport in which extremely <u>agile</u> people treat city landscapes as their obstacle course, throwing themselves across railings, walls and rooftops. It requires skill and courage rather than stamina.

Having helped set up the UK freerunning scene in his teens, Sticky was feted for his achievements. He was flown around the world to appear in advertising campaigns and teach movie stars how to do stunt work. His diary was full, and it appeared as though he had found an ideal existence, full of interest and excitement. His future seemed fixed. [2] He retreated to North Wales to live in a borrowed cottage and fulfill a secret mission: to become the first person to freerun over 1,000 miles, camping out each night in the countryside and <u>performing</u> parkour in the cities he travels through on the way.

'Freerunning involves working out the most efficient way of going from point A to point B through a process of trial and error,' says Budden. [3] 'You do some cool stuff over 20 metres and then you go back and do the same thing again. I wanted to push myself outside my comfort zone. It's about <u>overcoming</u> obstacles in my head.'

One particular incident that occurred the previous year had confirmed that he was ready for the <u>challenge</u>. He had been organising workshops for the Royal Marines, who wanted to use free-running techniques in combat situations. [4] 'It normally takes sixteen weeks to train up for these,' says Budden, 'and I got through them first time. That's when I realised I had <u>potential</u> I wasn't yet using.'

There's also something monastic about his life up here in the hills that wouldn't be out of place in a martial arts movie. The cottage he has been lent has no heating, just an open fire for which he must chop wood. Every day he rises at 7a.m., chooses a nearby mountain, and runs to the top. [5] Some days he sets himself extra tasks such as 1,000 squats, 200 chin-ups, or, if it has snowed overnight, to complete his run barefoot. But there's no hint of ego or vanity in his manner. He's far more interested in talking about the charity he's going to run for – the Motor Neurone Disease Association – than himself. He feels very strongly about what he's doing, and has no intention of giving up.

His girlfriend is very worried about his plan to attempt his run without a support vehicle and carrying a one-man tent on his back. 'She keeps saying, "You can't do it! You need a shower every night!"' [6] 'I'll just use the rivers,' he says. 'I still believe that to do free running you only need a pair of trainers and an open mind.' It's all about the attitude you have and the goals you set yourself.

3 **Complete sentences 1–6 with the underlined words from the article in Activity 2. Sometimes you need to change the form of the word.**

1 .... , the ability to do an activity for a long time, is developed in training.

2 When passing in football .... is just as important as speed.

3 She enjoyed the .... of the new job despite her fears of having so much responsibility.

4 Tina is just not realising her full .... She could do much better.

5 She had to .... her fear of public speaking.

6 As the audience leapt to their feet applauding loudly he realised he had given the most brilliant .... of his career.

4 **Match 1–6 with A–F.**

1 I try not to judge things too quickly –

2 I hate meeting a lot of new people.

3 I never get things right the first time.

4 He doesn't look over-confident,

5 I had no idea my friend was coming to visit,

6 It's easy to stick with things you're familiar with.

A It's a matter of trial and error.

B I prefer to push myself out of my comfort zone.

C she arrived completely out of the blue.

D there's no hint of such a feeling.

E I often feel out of place and uncomfortable.

F I like to keep an open mind.

5 **Choose the correct option in italics.**

1 The parcel arrived completely out of the *blue/ red/black* – I had no idea it was coming.

2 It's hard not to feel out of *area/place/room* at first when you arrive in a new town.

3 People who listen to others are usually keen to keep an open *thought/mind/view*.

4 I always like to have something to aim at in life – I try to *put/push/set* myself goals.

5 If you try hard but don't succeed, your efforts will have been all in *worth/vain/effort*.

6 Sometimes it's impossible to know what to do – it's a matter of *try/trial/tried* and error.

7 It's good to challenge yourself and not always stay in your comfort *place/area/zone*.

8 Successful people are good at *overcoming/ beating/climbing* obstacles they meet in life.

Grammar
mixed conditionals
▶ CB page 114

1 **Tick all the possible options to complete sentences 1–4.**

1 He would not be famous
- **A** if he were a typical sportsman.
- **B** if he had been a typical sportsman.
- **C** if he must have been a typical sportsman.

2 Please ask the teacher for our homework books
- **A** if you happened to see her.
- **B** if you will see her.
- **C** if you see her.

3 If I had seen the review in the newspaper earlier,
- **A** I would have gone to see the play.
- **B** I will go to see the play.
- **C** I would be at the play now.

4 If I'd left the party earlier,
- **A** I wouldn't be so tired now.
- **B** I won't be so tired now.
- **C** I won't have been so tired now.

2 **Complete sentences 1–8 with the most suitable form of the verbs in brackets. There may be more than one possible answer.**

1 If she only got on the plane an hour ago, she .... (*not be*) in Rome yet.

2 If I hadn't stayed out in the sun so long, I .... (*not be*) so burnt today.

3 I would have moved to Italy if I .... (*speak*) good Italian.

4 I'd feel much happier now if I .... (*meet*) Sue to discuss the problem yesterday.

5 If I'd started playing tennis when I was younger, I .... (*be*) a much better player now.

6 If you .... (*not come*) over tonight, we .... (*help*) each other with our homework now.

7 If you .... (*plan*) to withdraw a lot of money from the bank at one time, you .... (*need*) to notify them in advance.

8 If I ever .... (*want*) someone to talk to, he .... (*always be*) there for me.

3 **Find and correct the mistakes in the mixed conditional sentences.**

1 If I didn't spend so much money last Saturday, I would have more in my bank account now.

2 If I had been able to find a job in London, I wouldn't have lived in Paris now.

3 If I hadn't studied German for six years at school, I'm not so good at it now.

4 If I had worked harder, I was in a higher position in the company now.

5 If I could choose my name when I was born, I would be called Chloe now.

6 If I would win the lottery, I would give all the money away.

Vocabulary
prefixes that change meaning
▶ CB page 115

1 **Match prefixes 1–10 with meanings A–J.**

1	im-	**A**	again
2	hyper-	**B**	three
3	over-	**C**	between
4	inter-	**D**	more than usual
5	tri-	**E**	a negative idea
6	pre-	**F**	badly, wrongly
7	re-	**G**	before
8	dis-	**H**	not or opposite of
9	mis-	**I**	in favour of
10	pro-	**J**	too much

2 **Complete sentences 1–8 with prefixes from Activity 1.**

1 I'm trying to diet – I feel as though I'm just a bit ....weight.

2 The team has just set off to play in the ....national competition in the USA.

3 I've already read the book three times but I love it so much I'm going to ....read it.

4 My new car has a great radio with loads of ....set stations already in place.

5 Unfortunately I'm very ....organised – my flat is in a real mess!

6 My friend is a ....-athlete – he runs, swims and cycles long distances in the same race.

7 My nephew is ....active – he just rushes around all the time and I can't cope!

8 I'm sorry I went to the wrong place – I must have ....understood your message.

Use of English
Word formation (Part 3)
▶ CB page 115

1 For questions 1–8, read the text below. Use the word given in capitals at the end of some of the lines to form a word that fits in the gap in the same line. There is an example at the beginning (0).

A risk worth taking?

Are people going too far seeking new exploits to test their physical and mental **(0)** _capabilities_? One extreme sport is described as a **(1)** .... slide through rapids, followed by jumping off waterfalls and abseiling down cliffs. But are such sports too **(2)** .... ? It's the danger that attracts thrill-seekers and their **(3)** .... is that it's human nature to want to push forward the limits of achievement.

CAPABLE
DRAMA

CHALLENGE
ARGUE

Not everyone agrees. Critics have called for tighter controls on such sports, to avoid situations where **(4)** .... have to go to the aid of those who get injured. However, one man who went on an adventure trip has no regrets.

RESCUE

'Our **(5)** .... was of the utmost importance for those in charge. Luckily I also know my limitations and recognise my **(6)** .... Nevertheless, I believe it's important for everyone to **(7)** .... their horizons and set themselves new goals. An increase in the number of extreme sports is **(8)** .... to people turning into couch potatoes, just sitting and watching other people have fun!'

SAFE

EXPERIENCE

BROAD

PREFER

Listening
Multiple choice (Part 1)
▶ CB page 116

1 ▶ 22 **You will hear people talking in eight different situations. For each question, choose the best answer, A, B or C.**

1 You hear two friends talking about a newspaper article about a dog.
What do they agree about the article?
   A It was amusing for everyone to read.
   B It was irrelevant to everyday life.
   C It was an unusual topic for a newspaper article.

2 You hear a voicemail message a woman has left on your phone.
Why did the woman call?
   A to introduce a special offer
   B to explain a new phone contract
   C to clarify some confusing information

3 You hear two friends talking about shopping for clothes.
What do they both think about buying clothes?
   A It's acceptable to buy copies of branded clothes.
   B Desirable clothes always cost too much money.
   C Having cheap clothes only encourages people to buy more.

4 You overhear a man leaving a voicemail message.
What is he doing?
   A asking for confirmation of an arrangement
   B warning about a potential problem
   C recommending a place to eat

5 You hear two friends talking about a concert they've just been to.
How does the woman feel about it?
   A impressed by the standards of technology used
   B inspired by the reaction of the audience
   C happy with the quality of the venue

6 You hear part of an interview with a young dancer.
What did she find surprising when she joined a professional dance company?
   A how tiring the daily routine was
   B how supportive other company members were
   C how much preparation there was for a performance

7 You hear a young man talking about his first experience of rock climbing.
How does he feel about it?
   A dissatisfied with his level of ability
   B unsure about getting involved with a dangerous activity
   C unhappy about having to cope with difficult conditions

8 You hear two people talking about a new leisure centre.
What does the man think the centre should do?
   A provide more activities for younger children
   B restrict the opening hours to avoid annoying neighbours
   C offer more discounts to attract a wider clientele

Vocabulary
adjectives and verbs with prepositions
▶ CB page 117

1 Complete the text with suitable prepositions.

A great experience

I never thought I'd have the chance to go on an expedition to the North Pole – but I did, and although I was worried **(1)** .... the cold before I went it turned out to be a great experience. I was thrilled **(2)** .... having the chance to go, and I was determined **(3)** .... do well. The expedition was intended **(4)** .... people in good physical shape, and keen **(5)** .... pushing themselves physically and mentally – great, but it meant I had to be confident **(6)** .... my own level of fitness. I did a whole lot of training! We had to rely **(7)** .... cross-country skiing to cross the difficult terrain, which was very demanding, and we also needed to be able **(8)** .... pull a heavy sled (between 30 and 40 kilos) for several hours at a time. Towards the end of each day when we stopped skiing, it was critical that we had enough energy **(9)** .... set up camp, melt snow for hot tea or cocoa, and make dinner. The expedition leaders insisted **(10)** .... maintaining a spirit of support and teamwork, as dealing **(11)** .... such difficult weather conditions is very challenging. We didn't need to be world-class athletes to participate **(12)** .... this expedition but it was certainly challenging and my friends were very impressed **(13)** .... my achievement when I got back! This is an experience that will stay with me for the rest of my life and I'd love to be involved **(14)** .... another one before too long!

phrasal verbs with *off*
▶ CB page 117

2 Complete the sentences with phrasal verbs from the box in the correct form. There is one you don't need to use.

call off	cut off	go off	put off
see someone off	tell someone off		wear off

1 The trip was .... until the following day because of the rain.

2 The villagers were .... from the nearby town by the thick snow.

3 I love it when friends and family come to .... before a trip.

4 I felt so cold that my head ached, but after a while the pain ....

5 The expedition was .... completely because the weather was so bad.

6 If you break the safety rules you should expect to be ....

Grammar
hypothetical meaning
▶ CB page 118

1 Choose the correct option in italics to complete the sentences.

1 Tim really wishes he *runs/would have run/could run* in the next London Marathon but the doctor says he is not able to.

2 If only I *hadn't spent/wouldn't have spent/didn't spend* all my time watching TV instead of training!

3 I wish you *would take up/would have taken up/had taken up* a safer sport than parkour now that you are getting older.

4 If only your grandfather *would be/has been/were* alive to see you win the cup.

5 Don't you wish that you *had never started/would not start/did not start* this project?

6 I really wish I *could improve/improved/have improved* my agility and muscle endurance.

7 If only I *didn't live/wouldn't live/haven't lived* so far from the sea.

8 Eleanor wished she *has/would have/could have* joined the expedition to the Arctic Circle but her parents wouldn't let her go.

2 Find and correct the mistakes in sentences 1–4.

1 The film was so well made I felt as if I have actually climbed Mount Everest myself.

2 I'd rather you don't invite Jamie to the party. He doesn't get on very well with Max.

3 It's high time we had left for the station. We'll be lucky to catch the 9.30 train.

4 It was very silly of you to go out on your bike without a helmet. Suppose you fell off and hit your head?

Speaking
Long turn (Part 2)
▶ CB page 119

1 ▶ 23 Listen to the interlocutor's instructions and what one candidate said. Has she followed the instructions?

2 Look at the interlocutor's question to some other candidates. Match responses 1–4 with the examiner's comments A–D.

Interlocutor: Which of these two trips would you prefer to go on? Why?

1

> The second one.

2

> I would prefer to be the person on the bicycle. I would love to travel alone like that.

3

> No, I haven't, but I'd like to.

4

> I can see many nice things in these photographs. For example, it seems to me that these people must be very cold and I think the bicycle looks like a very expensive one and very fast.

A

> Misunderstood the question.

B

> Answer far too brief.

C

> Response too long and irrelevant.

D

> Good clear response.

Writing
Review (Part 2)
▶ CB page 120

1 Read the task below.

You see this announcement in an English language magazine.

Reviews of computer games wanted!

Have you played a computer game recently that you really liked?

Write a review, describing the game and explaining what you liked about it. Tell us whether or not you would recommend it to other people of your age.

2 In a review you use functions (describe, explain, give an opinion and recommend). Look at the words and phrases below and identify each function.

1 In my view … ....
2 What I mean is … ....
3 What happens is … ....
4 It seems to me that … ....
5 It's a fast-moving game with lots of action. ....
6 I enjoyed the speed of the game. ....
7 I can only suggest that you try it yourself. ....
8 It's not to be missed! ....

3 Read the review below. Which functions (describe, explain, give an opinion, recommend) does the writer use in each paragraph?

I've been playing *Demon warriors* for the last few months, and it's pretty awesome. It's a game with different levels, and you have to collect special tokens as you play so that you can progress to the next level. There are some great sets, which are very colourful, thrilling music and, of course, there are lots of things like monsters to stop you getting there!

What I like about it is the variety. Although some people could get irritated if they can't move on, it is designed in such a way as to be challenging. This means that when you do well it makes you feel really good. You can also play it with friends, so there's a competitive element to it.

It's not a cheap game, which might put some people off. But in my view it's worth the money, as it gives you hours of fun. I would certainly suggest that you try it yourself!

4 Find words in the review in Activity 3 that mean the same as these words.

1 fantastic ....
2 move up ....
3 exciting ....
4 annoyed ....
5 planned ....
6 factor ....

5 Now write your own answer to the task in Activity 1. Try to use a variety of interesting language. Write 140–190 words.

12 Crime scene

Listening
Sentence completion (Part 2)
▶ CB page 122

1 Choose the correct options in italics to complete the sentences.

1 I read crime novels because I love *solving/working* problems.
2 It's important to *make/do* research before writing a book.
3 It's useful when tips are *passed on/given on* by successful writers.
4 People love *going through/getting out* clues to a crime.
5 Writers can waste a lot of time waiting for inspiration to *hit/strike*.
6 A good cover will *grab/take* people's attention and make them pick up the book.

2 ▶ 24 **You will hear a young crime writer called Carrie Thomas talking to a group of students about her life and work. For questions 1–10, complete the sentences with a word or short phrase.**

Carrie says that writing crime fiction is not a **(1)** .... that anyone can learn.

Carrie uses the word **(2)** .... to describe how she feels when she can't write.

Carrie advises would-be crime writers to be sure of their personal **(3)** .... for wanting to be a writer.

Before she started writing, Carrie found out about the **(4)** .... used in police departments.

Carrie suggests analysing other writers' books to see what makes their books **(5)** .... and why they make money.

Carrie compares crime novels to **(6)** .... to explain why people like them.

Carrie appreciated being told not to forget the **(7)** .... of crime writing and to stick to the conventions.

Carrie says it is important to take the advice of an **(8)** .... when writing.

Carrie says that the synopsis of the book on the dust jacket must be interesting but **(9)** .... as well.

According to Carrie, successful authors must be good at **(10)** .... which may come as a surprise to new writers.

Grammar
obligation, prohibition and necessity
▶ CB page 123

1 Choose the correct options in italics to complete the sentences.

1 He *shouldn't/mustn't* have told John about the misunderstanding because it just caused trouble.
2 You *needn't/mustn't* drive me to the station as it's only a five-minute walk.
3 You *need/must* read that new crime thriller – it's really good.
4 We're not *allowed to/supposed to* speak to the newspapers about the case, though it's not actually forbidden.
5 I *need/must* to go to the dentist's this afternoon, so I'll have to miss the meeting.
6 You *mustn't/don't have to* say anything if you're arrested.

2 **Find and correct the mistakes in sentences 1–8. Tick the sentences that are correct.**

Did you have

0 ⟨to give evidence after the accident?

1 She had leave home early to make sure she didn't miss the meeting.

2 The teacher told me I needn't do the test again because my marks were good enough.

3 You are not allowed driving at over 70 mph.

4 You must to try not to get depressed – we know you're innocent.

5 Witnesses may think they don't have to telling the truth to the judge, but they do.

6 You are not allowed to drink and drive – it's illegal.

7 You mustn't do the washing-up; it's not necessary because I can do it later.

8 You shouldn't smoke anywhere in public buildings.

3 **For questions 1–6, complete the second sentence so that it has a similar meaning to the first sentence, using the word given. Do not change the word given. You must use between two and five words, including the word given.**

1 It's all right if members bring guests to the gym on Monday evenings.

   ALLOWED

   Members .... guests to the gym on Monday evenings.

2 The police insisted that he paid the fine on time.

   HAD

   He .... the fine on time because the police insisted.

3 The robber was not obliged to meet his victim to apologise, but he did.

   NEED

   The robber .... meet his victim to apologise, but he did.

4 Is it really necessary for me to make a statement now?

   HAVE

   Do .... make a statement now?

5 I'm working late tonight as they've asked me if I can hand in this report tomorrow.

   SUPPOSED

   I'm working late tonight as .... hand in this report tomorrow.

6 They say I'm not allowed to smoke anywhere in the building.

   MUST

   They say .... anywhere in the building.

Speaking
Discussion (Part 4)
▶ CB page 124

1 **Read what students said in answer to a discussion question. Underline where the student:**

1 gives examples. (find four examples)

2 tries to include the other candidate in the discussion. (find three examples)

3 uses phrases for agreeing and disagreeing. (find four examples)

I = Interlocutor, G = Günther, M = Manoela

I: How has the public's awareness of cybercrime changed?

G: I think people are far more conscious of the risks than they were a few years ago. For example, if they're shopping online and need to pay for something with a credit card, most people know they should only do this if it's a site they can trust. Otherwise, they run the risk of identity theft. Would you agree?

M: I certainly would, particularly after what happened to my mother. She's a bit careless about things like that. A couple of weeks ago she had a problem because someone had got hold of her credit card details and had tried to book a train ticket somewhere in France. Has anything like that ever happened to you?

G: No, fortunately. But sometimes I wonder if there is such a thing as a secure site. After all, we're constantly hearing that confidential information has been leaked from a site because of hacking. Even mobile phones aren't safe.

M: No, they're not. I get a lot of unwanted messages on mine. But what about social networking sites? I think they can be very risky. Something really horrible happened to a friend of mine, for instance. Another boy created a page using his name and said all sorts of terrible things about him and his friends.

G: If he managed to find out who it was, he could sue him for libel.

M: It was someone in our class at school who was always insulting my friend and calling him names. It turned out he'd posted pictures of another friend of ours without asking her permission and also tried to get a lot of people to put insulting comments on her wall. My friend was partly to blame, though. She should have checked the privacy settings on the site so that people who were not her friends wouldn't have access. Everyone should do that, don't you think?

G: Yes and no. I mean, it's also quite good if old friends can find you and get in touch.

Vocabulary
shopping online
▶ CB page 125

1 **Complete the sentences with the words in the box. There is one word you don't need to use.**

credit	password	register	retailers
safeguard	software	service	

1 Some people find it difficult to avoid .... card scams online.

2 Established .... are trusted more than pop-up shops.

3 It's important to choose a strong .... to keep your accounts online safe.

4 Be careful to .... your personal information online.

5 It's often necessary to .... your personal details before you can buy anything on a website.

6 Choose a reliable .... provider when you set up an account on the internet.

word formation
▶ CB page 125

2 **Correct the mistake with word formation in each sentence.**

1 Shopping online is very convenience – I love it!

2 It's very important to keep your pin number security.

3 Some shopping sites have links to other sites, so you have to protect your private.

4 Many scams look very profession so you have to be careful.

5 Make sure you have taken the right secure measures to protect your data.

6 Make sure you close your browse window after you have finished shopping.

Reading
Multiple choice (Part 5)
▶ CB page 126

1 **You are going to read an article about a stolen bicycle. Read the article once and decide if the following statement is true or false.**

The woman took the bicycle because she believed it was hers.

2 **Read the article again. For questions 1–6, choose the answer (A, B, C or D) which you think fits best according to the text.**

1 What made it easier for the thieves to steal the writer's bike?

A They knew it had been left unlocked.

B They knew no one would see them.

C They had a special tool.

D They had plenty of time.

2 Why was the writer frustrated with the response from the police?

A She thought it was their duty to go with her to the market.

B She didn't think they believed she could find her bike at the market.

C She didn't think they had given her good advice.

D She thought they were being deliberately uncooperative.

3 How did the writer feel when she realised her bike was not in the white van?

A Relieved because she would not have been brave enough to speak to the man.

B Afraid because the man might have seen her watching him.

C Worried because she didn't know where else her bike could be.

D Hopeful because she thought she might find it in another van.

4 The writer thinks the boy gave her the bike because

A he saw how angry she was.

B he knew it was stolen.

C he thought she was going to pay him.

D he realised she was bigger than him.

5 What does 'there' in line 49 refer to?

A among the crowds

B between the stalls

C with the boy

D just behind the writer

6 How does the writer feel now?

A annoyed about having to repair her bike

B sorry for having made a mistake

C relieved to have her bike back

D guilty about what she did

THE DAY I STOLE A BICYCLE

It was my first brand new bike. Nothing fancy – the cheapest Ridgeback on the market – but I was really proud of it and I loved it.

Two months later, on a sunny Saturday afternoon, I locked it up on Whitechapel High Street in London. There were lots of people about. I felt sure it would be fine, but two hours later, it was gone. The lock was lying on the pavement. It had been cut straight through with a pair of bolt cutters. I was <u>gutted</u>.

I felt sure it would turn up at Brick Lane Market the next day and tried to arrange to meet the police there so that we could look for it together and reclaim it, but they told me that they couldn't go along with me. They were very sympathetic and said that if I was to find my bike I should ring 999 and they'd <u>be straight over</u>. I didn't want to argue but I couldn't see how that was going to help. The market would be crowded and my bike would <u>be long gone</u> in the time it took them to reach me.

I got to the market early. At the far end of the street a particularly <u>scary-looking</u> man was directing two others who were unloading bikes from a white van. He had his back to me and he was shaven-headed and absolutely huge. I knew if my bike came out the back of that van, I'd be going home to save up for another one without saying a word, but I watched anyway. I was almost glad that my silver Ridgeback didn't appear, though lots of other bikes did. There were other vans but my bike didn't come out of those either.

By ten o'clock I'd been at the market for over two hours and it was getting crowded. The white vans had stopped coming but bikes were still arriving ridden by teenagers. This is where I saw my bike – my <u>pristine</u>, two-month-old silver ladies' Ridgeback – except now it had a <u>buckled</u> front wheel and it was missing a seat post. I couldn't tell how old the boy holding it was but I was relieved that he was smaller than me. I was scared but angry enough to go ahead and speak to him. I asked him how much he wanted. He said £90. I told him that it was my bike and he could either give it to me or he could wait for the police to arrive and I would show them my receipt. He gave it to me, turned around and walked away.

I took a deep breath and started to wheel my unrideable bike through what were now thick crowds between the stalls. When I had confronted the boy I had noticed a man watching us from the other side of the narrow street. The boy had walked off in his direction. As I looked over my shoulder, I could see this man was now behind me in the crowds. I kept walking but every time I looked over my shoulder the man was still there. We both knew that he was going to <u>catch up with</u> me as soon as I crossed the road. I couldn't see that there was anything else for me to do. I got on the bike and rode it, with its <u>wobbly</u> wheel and no seat post – but I didn't care. I just needed to get away from this man who I believed was intent on doing me harm. I made eye contact with the man chasing me once more as I clanked away down the street. He had stopped following me. He took one good sour look at my face and turned around to walk back into the market.

line 49

I made it home <u>in one piece</u> and, after a deep breath and a cup of tea, flipped my bike over to remove the buckled front wheel. Here comes the <u>shameful</u> part. This is when I checked the serial number against my receipt and realised that this wasn't my bike after all. It was the same make and colour but it wasn't mine. I kept it anyway.

---

3 **Match the underlined words and phrases in the article in Activity 2 with definitions 1–10.**

1 undamaged and clean
2 moving from side to side in an unsteady way
3 have disappeared a long time before
4 very upset and disappointed
5 deserving blame

6 come immediately
7 with a frightening appearance
8 bent
9 unhurt
10 come from behind and reach someone in front of you

Use of English
Open cloze (Part 2)
▶ CB page 128

1 Read crime stories 1–2. A student has made mistakes filling in some of the gaps. Find the mistakes and correct them.

1

> A burglar was trapped after he fell **(1)** down a chimney while trying to climb over the roof of a house he had just **(2)** breaked into.
>
> Police arrested the man after **(3)** been called out by the owners of the house who heard his cries **(4)** for help.
>
> The man had tried to escape out of a window in the roof with his bag of cash and jewellery, but fell in the dark and **(5)** get stuck inside the chimney.

2

> A man went into a drug store, pulled **(6)** up a gun from his pocket and announced that the store was **(7)** being robbed. He pulled a paper bag over his head **(8)** as a facemask. He immediately realised that he'd forgotten to cut eyeholes in the bag and so he couldn't see anything. He **(9)** had arrested by security men that he hadn't seen standing **(10)** on the corner of the store.

2 For questions 1–8, read the text below and think of the word which best fits each gap. Use only one word in each gap. There is an example at the beginning (0).

Are you helping criminals?

We all send them, thinking that we **(0)** need to keep in touch with others about our movements. But **(1)** .... much might we actually be revealing in our out-of-office email messages? A careless, frivolous message conveys a sloppy, unprofessional image. But **(2)** .... you think that's bad, think again. Let me give you **(3)** .... example. Last week I got 135 automated emails. Of these, twenty gave away information about clients and projects and twenty-seven were insecure, leaving the sender open to cybercrime.

How does it work? Apparently **(4)** .... cyber criminals do is send thousands of emails completely **(5)** .... random. Once they get your automatic response, they can find out personal details, even possibly **(6)** .... you live, by cross-referencing the information. An automatic message can alert thieves to the fact that you are away, and the chance of someone breaking **(7)** .... your house in your absence is increased.

So include the minimum of information on your automated message, **(8)** .... 'I am unable to deal with your email at the moment'. Don't help criminals by telling them too much!

3 Complete the sentences with a reflexive pronoun.

1 My friends always enjoy .... when they visit my house.
2 My sister was so good at tennis that she liked to compare .... to professional players.
3 I often go shopping by .... because I find it easier to choose what to buy.
4 My boss always introduces .... to new members of staff – he's very friendly.
5 It's always better to try clothes on .... before you buy them – it's no good relying on pictures online.
6 My family and I go shopping together every week – we enjoy .... in the shopping mall.

Grammar
have/get something done
▶ CB page 129

1 Complete the conversation with the prompts in brackets. Make sure you use the correct tense of the verbs.

J = José, K = Karin

J: Why is Elena looking so worried?

K: She **(1)** .... (bicycle, steal) last week when she went to the market.

J: Oh, no! What's she going to do about it?

K: Well, amazingly enough she **(2)** .... (it, return) to her already. She found it outside her house this morning, or at least she thought it was her bicycle.

J: What do you mean?

K: There's a problem. It's the same make but it's a different colour. She thought the thieves **(3)** .... (it, repaint) so that it would be more difficult to identify.

J: So is she **(4)** .... (it, painted) silver like it used to be?

K: She was going to, but then she discovered that one of the wheels was buckled and she took it to the bike shop to **(5)** .... (it, repair).

J: What happened?

K: Well, in the bike shop they asked to see her receipt and when they checked the serial number on the receipt and compared it to the one on the bike, they didn't match. She **(6)** .... (it, fix) anyway but she took it to the police station.

Writing
Report (Part 2)
▶ CB page 130

1 Look at the task. Which three of the following do students not have to do in their report?

> The director of the college where you study is concerned about security, and is planning to either put security cameras in the college or install new devices for students to lock up their bicycles. As there is not much money to spend, the director has asked students to write a report assessing the value of both ideas and recommending which one most students would find useful.
>
> **Write your report.**

1 Describe both ideas.
2 Consider the advantages and disadvantages of each idea.
3 Describe security arrangements in the college.
4 Explain the opinions of other students.
5 Recommend one idea.
6 Give reasons for recommendations.
7 Think of a new idea to recommend.
8 Explain the purpose of the report.

2 Rewrite the sentences with the correct form of the word in brackets.

1 I suggest .... (*spend*) money on security cameras.
2 It is recommended that students .... (*fill in*) a questionnaire.
3 My suggestion would be .... (*consult*) as many people as possible.
4 I recommend the director .... (*ask*) students for their opinions.
5 It is my suggestion that students should be able .... (*lock up*) their bikes.
6 I recommend .... (*talk*) to students about this.

3 Read the report opposite that was written in answer to the task in Activity 1 and do the following:

1 Underline two pieces of unnecessary information the student has included.
2 Correct ten mistakes with spelling and grammar.
3 Choose a heading for each paragraph A–F. There are two headings you do not need to use.

A Introduction
B Ideas from students
C Recommendations
D The cost of suggestions
E Locking devices for bicycles
F Security cameras

....

The purpose of this report is to asess the value of improving security by either putting security cameras into the college or providing devices to allow students to lock up their bicycles. I consulted many students, and this report is based in their responses.

....

Students felt there would be an overall benefit in instaling security cameras, but it could turn up to be expensive. The cameras in the new shopping centre cost a fortune! In addition, someone must watch the screens, which seems a waste of time and money.

....

It is a big problem for everyone when bicycles stolen, as many students come to college by bikes. At the moment they leave them at the entrance, but several have been stolen. Last week a red one was taken. It would not being very expensive to install bicycle racks in front of the college, and students were liking this idea.

....

Based on the views expressed by students, and on the fact that cameras would be expensive, I recommend install devices for students to lock up their bicycles. This would encourage even more students cycling which is good for the environment and also for the health and fitness of students.

4 Write your own answer to the task below. Remember to make recommendations, giving good reasons for your suggestions. Write 140–190 words.

> You have recently been on a holiday where several things went wrong. You lost your wallet and some jewellery was stolen from your hotel room. The manager of the hotel has asked you to write a report for the hotel security team. You should explain what happened, and say how you think security at the hotel could be improved.

Multiple-choice cloze (Part 1)

For questions 1–8, read the text below and decide which answer (A, B, C or D) best fits each gap. There is an example at the beginning (0).

An escapist read!

This book **(0)** A. kept me enthralled for a whole weekend. It describes an incident in which a scientist was standing on top of a Colombian volcano when it erupted, killing several of his colleagues **(1)** .... He tried to scramble down the incredibly steep side of the volcano, but was caught by a heavy shower of white-hot rocks. Several of these hit him, **(2)** .... him so badly that he feared he would not survive. However, **(3)** .... the dangers, two very brave women **(4)** .... an extraordinary rescue, and helped him to safety.

This book describes the work of scientists who place themselves in danger in the search to understand volcanoes, and shows why they choose to **(5)** .... such risks. They hope to develop the technique of **(6)** .... accurately when the next eruption might occur **(7)** .... to give people living in the area **(8)** .... warning which would save lives. It is a thought-provoking and fascinating book, which I recommend.

0	**A** kept	**B** held	**C** got	**D** made
1	**A** actually	**B** directly	**C** instantly	**D** momentarily
2	**A** damaging	**B** injuring	**C** spoiling	**D** smashing
3	**A** despite	**B** even	**C** providing	**D** consequently
4	**A** took up	**B** made up	**C** set out	**D** carried out
5	**A** get	**B** take	**C** have	**D** do
6	**A** planning	**B** forecasting	**C** projecting	**D** viewing
7	**A** so that	**B** in order	**C** in case	**D** though
8	**A** future	**B** ahead	**C** advance	**D** before

Open cloze (Part 2)

For questions 9–16, read the text below and think of the word which best fits each gap. Use only one word in each gap. There is an example at the beginning (0).

Cheerleading may be riskier than sport!

Cheerleading **(0)** has become a mainstream activity – many sports would be nothing today without groups of chanting young people dancing on the sidelines. But would you believe that showing support for a team **(9)** .... this way may be almost as risky as playing the game **(10)** .... ? Each season, just as the players undergo trials for their sport, young people try out for their cheerleading team, hoping to join that elite group of people **(11)** .... spend the game urging their team on to greater efforts. What they do during the game is a key factor in creating an atmosphere within a stadium. In the past, cheerleading **(12)** .... to be fun, but now it may have a darker side. Cheerleading once simply involved performing a simple routine while at the same time making a lot of noise. But now it's turned into serious gymnastics and is competitive in its **(13)** .... right. Each season thousands of young people strive to come **(14)** .... with the most dramatic display of choreography they can, and as **(15)** .... result they end up needing emergency hospital treatment. Although sport itself is well-regulated, cheerleading is **(16)** .... , so maybe what it now needs are some serious rules!

Word formation (Part 3)

For questions 17–24, read the text below. Use the word given in capitals at the end of some of the lines to form a word that fits in the gap in the same line. There is an example at the beginning (0).

Mountain storm nightmare

A young couple had a **(0)** _miraculous_ escape during a back-packing holiday in the mountains. Sally and Chris found themselves stranded in freezing conditions, surrounded by sheer rock faces in every **(17)** .... They tried to call the emergency services, but to their horror discovered they were **(18)** .... to get a signal. They made the difficult **(19)** .... to camp where they were and wait for morning, even though the weather was appalling. As daylight approached, Sally knew that she was **(20)** .... of climbing down unaided and Chris set off to find help alone. Hours passed until she heard a helicopter in the distance, and waved **(21)** .... to attract the pilot's attention. She was taken to hospital where she learnt that Chris had fallen during his descent due to the **(22)** .... conditions, and been forced to crawl for hours before reaching a small village. After an **(23)** .... reunion, the couple decided to choose less **(24)** .... holidays in future!

MIRACLE	
DIRECT	
ABLE	
DECIDE	
CAPABLE	
FRANTIC	
ICE	
EMOTION	
ADVENTURE	

Key word transformation (Part 4)

For questions 25–30, complete the second sentence so that it has a similar meaning to the first sentence, using the word given. Do not change the word given. You must use between two and five words, including the word given.

Here is an example (0).

Example:

0 A very friendly woman gave us directions when we got lost.

GIVEN

When we got lost we _were given directions by_ a very friendly woman.

25 I prefer playing football to tennis.

RATHER

I .... tennis.

26 Do you think I have to get a visa to visit the country?

NECESSARY

Do you think .... to get a visa to visit the country?

27 If no one turns up for the meeting, you can go home.

LONG

You can go home, ... turns up for the meeting.

28 If it isn't too cold, we'll go skiing tomorrow.

UNLESS

We'll go skiing tomorrow .... too cold.

29 The plane was so crowded that I couldn't sleep on the long flight.

TOO

The plane was .... sleep on the long flight.

30 'Don't leave the building without locking up, John,' said the manager.

LEAVING

The manager reminded John .... the building.

Common errors: B2 First

Strategy:
In the exam you need to be aware of strategies that will help you with the exam tasks. Here are some tips for approaching each paper and examples of common mistakes students might make.

Use of English
General advice

- In Parts 1–3, read the title and text first to clarify the type/style of words required.
- Read the instructions – they tell you the text type and how many words to write.
- Check your spelling, as all words in Parts 1–4 must be correct.

Part 1: Multiple-choice cloze

1 **Match pieces of advice 1–3 with reasons A–C.**

1 Read the words before and after the gap before choosing your answer.
2 Think what the answer might be before you read the options.
3 Read the whole sentence before choosing an answer.

A This part often tests collocations, which may come before or after the gap.
B If the missing word is a linking word, you must understand the meaning of the whole sentence.
C You may already know the answer, so you can confirm this when you read the options.

2 **Look at the extract from a Part 1 task below. The student chose options 1D and 2A, which are wrong. Which piece of advice has he/she forgotten? What are the correct answers?**

There are different ways of achieving a happy life, including finding job satisfaction and experiencing enriching family relationships. However, **(1)** .... to what people might predict, some experts claim that simply enjoying yourself is not actually a priority. **(2)** .... other factors such as accepting responsibility and high self-esteem have to be equally important.

1 **A** against **B** opposing **C** contrary **D** contrast
2 **A** On top of that **B** So that **C** In that case **D** Since then

Part 2: Open cloze

3 **Match pieces of advice 1–3 with reasons A–C.**

1 Don't write a word in a gap before you have read the whole sentence.
2 Don't write more than one word.
3 Never write contractions such as *didn't* in a gap.

A These count as two words and will be wrong.
B You may miss the need for a negative, or a linking word like 'however'.
C Even if you think more than one answer is possible, you must only write one.

4 Look at the extract from a Part 2 task below. The student has written his/her answers, which are wrong. Which piece of advice has he/she forgotten? What are the correct answers?

> It's sometimes claimed that there is a special relationship between people and animals, and there are colourful anecdotes of people in difficulty being helped to safety by wild animals. However, **(1)** _supposing/if_ such improbable tales were actually true, would this mean that all animals are aware of humans and are standing by **(2)** _in order to_ offer a helping hand – or paw?

Part 3: Word formation

5 Match pieces of advice 1–3 with reasons A–C.

1 Always change the word in capitals.

2 Think about the grammar of the sentence and the missing word.

3 Read the whole sentence, not just the line, before changing the word.

A This will help you decide whether you need a noun, adjective, adverb, etc.

B You will not be able to use the word in the same form as the word in capitals.

C This will help you spot suffixes, prefixes, negatives and plurals.

6 Look at the extract from a Part 3 task below. Which piece of advice has the student forgotten? What is the correct answer?

> If you're someone who's terrified of heights, you may not want to try zip-lining. Although it's great fun, it's definitely **(8)** _suitable_ for anyone who has a phobia like that.   **SUIT**

Part 4: Key word transformation

7 Match pieces of advice 1–3 with reasons A–C.

1 Keep your sentence as close as possible to the meaning of the original.

2 Don't rewrite more than necessary or make up details.

3 Never change the given word, but remember to include it in your answer.

A You must think of a structure that contains the given word.

B You are being tested on your ability to paraphrase.

C If you write more than five words, you have made a mistake so go back and check.

8 Look at the question from a Part 4 task below. Which piece of advice has the student forgotten? What is the correct answer?

> I had never seen a glacier before I went to Norway.
>
> I
>
> When I was in Norway _I was thrilled to see a glacier for_ the first time.

Reading
General advice

- Read different things in English, as there are different types of text in Paper 1.
- Read all the rubrics (instructions) carefully to identify the type of text and the topic.
- Read the title of the text, which introduces the topic.

Part 5: Multiple choice (long text)

1 Match pieces of advice 1–3 with reasons A–C.

1 Read all the options carefully, especially if you must complete a sentence.

2 Be careful if you see the same word in the option and the text.

3 Think about what the text is actually saying.

A This does not mean it is the correct answer.

B Incorrect options may not reflect the true meaning of the text accurately.

C Each option may be true, but only one completes the sentence or answers the question correctly.

2 Look at the extract from a Part 5 task below. The student chose option B, which is wrong. Which piece of advice has he/she forgotten? What is the correct answer?

> Week two was harder. On two Huel meals a day I started to really miss eating. I love cooking and eating is a highly social occasion for me. But when I did sit down to a proper meal, I savoured every single mouthful. Huel had heightened my appreciation for food. Most encouragingly though, I was feeling great. There was no difference in energy levels at the gym and my body tolerated it well.
>
> **5** How did things change for the author in week two?
>   **A** She started to do more exercise.
>   **B** She gained a feeling of extra energy.
>   **C** She wanted to give up her experiment.
>   **D** She found what she ate more enjoyable.

Part 6: Gapped text

3 Match pieces of advice 1–3 with reasons A–C.

1 Read the sentences immediately before and after each gap carefully.

2 Read the main text before reading the missing sentences, and reread after doing the task.

3 Make sure linking words, tenses and time references in the main text match your choice of option.

A This helps you predict what kind of information is missing.

B This helps you understand text structure and topic, so you can check that your answers make sense.

C Words like *firstly, last night, those, its* identify sequence and references and help you make your choice.

4 Look at the extract and some of the options from a Part 6 task below. The student chose sentence C from the options, which is wrong. Which piece of advice has he/she forgotten? What is the correct answer?

Writing a successful pop song might not seem too complicated at first glance. After all, it just takes two or three short verses, repeated choruses, a couple of hooks and a good melody, all wrapped up in about three minutes. But just take a look at the credits for any typical contemporary hit. [1] One recent number one single was the result of the work of five writers, two producers and a remixer. The current top ten features forty different writers and nineteen producers. Nowadays, it certainly seems to be a case of the more the merrier.

B One way record companies manage to do this is by including producers as part of song-writing teams.

C But somewhere along the line that all changed.

D You will see that huge teams of people are involved in its creation.

Part 7: Multiple matching

5 Match pieces of advice 1–3 with reasons A–C.

1 First, read the texts very quickly, but don't spend a lot of time on them.

2 Second, read all the options carefully and scan the texts to find each answer.

3 Be careful if you see the same word in the text and in the question.

A You should look out for paraphrases, not the identical word.

B You only need to get a general idea of what they are about.

C Different texts have similar information, but only one text matches each option.

6 Look at the extract and some of the options from a Part 7 task below. The student chose option 1, which is wrong. Which piece of advice has he/she forgotten? What is the correct answer?

Which person

was very unhappy before he started working from home?	1	
had to control the amount of time he was spending on work?	2	
likes to spend longer in bed in the mornings?	3	

C Mervin: musical supplier

I am the UK's leading supplier of music rolls for mechanical organs. F‹ me working from home has all the usual advantages like not having to g up at some ungodly hour to go out to work, especially when it's freezir outside; no office politics, no boss looking over my shoulder and I can s in the garden with my wife when the sun comes out. I can't think of ar disadvantages but there are some things to take into account. Firstly, home-based business sometimes has less credibility than a 'proper' on

Writing
General advice

* Read the question carefully and make sure that your answer is relevant.

* Use paragraphing and clear linking words to make your writing easy to follow.

* Check grammar and spelling – mistakes have a negative effect on the target reader.

* Use a style of language that is suitable for the person you are writing to.

Part 1: Compulsory question

1 Match pieces of advice 1–4 with reasons A–D.

1 Don't copy the same words from the question.

2 Make sure you include both the content points you are given.

3 Think of your own idea for the last point to support your argument.

4 Use an appropriate style of language.

A It is important to have one good idea of your own.

B They may be too informal for an essay.

C You must make a clear argument using the ideas you are given and one of your own.

D An essay should be written in a semi-formal style.

COMMON ERRORS: B2 FIRST

2 Look at the essay task on page 17 and read the short extract from a student's answer. Which piece of advice has the student forgotten?

> It's great to grow up in a large family because there are always lots of people to talk to and do stuff with. It's another fantastic bonus to have people to ask for advice, and that helps a lot.

Part 2

3 Match pieces of advice 1–4 with reasons A–D.

1 Choose the type of writing you are best at.
2 Allow enough time for Part 2. Don't rush through it.
3 Make a short plan before you start writing.
4 Expand on your ideas using a variety of vocabulary and structures.

A This helps you organise your answer and check you have enough relevant ideas.
B This gives you the chance to show how good you are.
C All questions carry equal marks in the Writing paper.
D This makes your writing interesting for the reader.

4 Look at the task and the short extract from a student's article below. Which piece of advice has the student forgotten?

> We're looking for articles on the best place to live – town or country. Send us an article describing where you live, saying why you like living there and explaining whether it's better to live in a town or the country.

> It is much nicer to live in the country. There are nice trees, flowers and animals. The city is not nice it is busy and noisy. In the country it is easy to be nice and quiet. The city traffic is hard and it is difficult to move around. In the country it is nice and easy to move around.

Listening
General advice

- Read and also listen to the instructions, as they give you context and introduce each topic.
- Don't worry about understanding everything you hear – concentrate on the task.
- Answer all the questions – there is no negative marking, so guess if you are not sure.

Part 1: Multiple choice (short extracts)

1 Match pieces of advice 1–3 with reasons A–C.

1 Remember the extracts are separate and not connected.
2 Don't spend too much time worrying about each answer.
3 Read the question carefully and identify key words such as *feel*, *think* and *why*.

A You may miss the next extract if you don't move on.
B This means if you are unsure of one answer, put something then wait for the next extract.
C The question for each extract has a different focus, e.g. feeling, opinion, purpose.

2 Look at the extract from a Part 1 task below. The student chose option A, which is wrong. Which piece of advice has he/she forgotten? What is the correct answer?

> You hear part of a radio phone-in programme.
> Why has the woman called the programme?
> **A** to complain about something
> **B** to clarify some facts
> **C** to make a suggestion

> *Thanks for finally having me on – I've been waiting absolutely ages! But at least I can have my say now. I've been listening for the last hour and I can't believe what your callers are saying. They must know that whatever anyone does on the recycling front – big or small – makes a difference. We're all responsible for the world we live in – how can they moan about being asked to put rubbish in different bins? But I accept that not everyone sees it like that, so what I think is that we should be given incentives to do it – that would get people on our side, and it would be pretty easy to put into operation I'd have thought.*

Part 2: Sentence completion

3 Match pieces of advice 1–3 with reasons A–C.

1 Read through all the sentences first.
2 Read what is written before and after each gap.
3 Listen carefully to the exact words used on the recording.

A This shows you the structure of the recording and helps you follow it.
B You must write the exact word you hear in the gap, not a paraphrase.
C This helps you identify the kind of information that is missing.

4 Look at the short extract from a Part 2 task below. The student has written his/her answer, which is wrong. Which piece of advice has he/she forgotten? What is the correct answer?

> Steve likes going **(1)** ~~walking~~ and rock-climbing in his spare time.
>
> *I also love adventure. My favourite leisure activities include going rock-climbing and hiking and once I started travelling round the world to remote places like rainforests and deserts I got completely hooked on the plight of endangered animals and ways of trying to save them.*

Part 3: Multiple matching

5 Match pieces of advice 1–3 with reasons A–C.

1 Check each option carefully when you listen and make your choice.

2 Don't be distracted if you hear the exact word you see in one of the options.

3 If you are unsure of an answer, note down your idea and confirm it on the second listening.

A You should be listening for gist and paraphrases of ideas.

B If you get one wrong, this may affect your other answers.

C Make sure that the one you have chosen is actually what the speaker means.

6 Look at the extract and some of the options from a Part 3 task below. The student chose option A, which is wrong. Which piece of advice has he/she forgotten? What is the correct answer?

> Why did the speaker choose their career?
> **A** following a parent's example
> **B** pursuing a dream
> **C** finding the salary attractive
>
> **Speaker 1**
>
> *I got interested in the whole area of sport when I started school, though I'd loved playing with a ball from a very early age. My parents always encouraged me, though I think they regarded it as a hobby rather than an actual career – we didn't know what the opportunities were then. I went on adventure holidays where sporting activities were top of my list, but it wasn't until I talked to a careers advisor that I realised how many possibilities sport offered apart from playing, and more importantly, how much money I could earn! That's when I decided I wanted to become a personal trainer.*

Part 4: Multiple choice (long text)

7 Match pieces of advice 1–3 with reasons A–C.

1 Check that the option you choose really matches the unfinished sentence or question.

2 Check the question and answer stems for key words and phrases such as *feel*, *the first time, too, most*.

3 Think about whether you are listening for gist, attitude, opinion or facts.

A These words will help you to listen for the right thing by giving you the time sequence.

B The options may be correct, but not answer the question asked.

C Understanding what to listen for focuses you on the information you need.

8 Look at the extract from a Part 4 task below. The student chose option A, which is wrong. Which piece of advice has he/she forgotten? What is the correct answer?

> When he started the trip, Alan
> **A** found it too physically demanding.
> **B** was upset by difficulties with the boat.
> **C** worried about the prospect of loneliness.
>
> *There's a gap between imagining something and doing it! Those first days were the hardest, 'cos there were loads of technical problems which got me down – I even thought I might have to give up! That would've been disappointing, but I carried on, sleeping in periods of twenty to forty minutes, eating rehydrated meals. Some people said I'd be lonely, but my mates had put loads of music on my iPod which was great. I'd stuck photos everywhere and packed loads of clothes so I didn't need to worry about doing washing!*

Speaking
General advice

- Listen carefully to instructions given by the interlocutor throughout the test.
- Ask the interlocutor to repeat instructions or questions if you are not sure.
- Speak clearly so that both the assessor and the interlocutor can hear you.

Part 1: Interview

1 **Match pieces of advice 1–3 with reasons A–C.**

1 Don't prepare long speeches in advance.

2 Practise talking about different topics in English.

3 Give some details but not so many that your answer takes too long.

A This will give you confidence.

B You won't answer questions appropriately and may include irrelevant information.

C Your answers should be suitable for a social situation, and not too long.

2 **Look at the question and answer below. Which piece of advice has the student forgotten?**

A: *Do you ever listen to the radio?*

B: *I think that people watch too much television these days and not many people listen to the radio, but the radio is good for concentrating on facts and getting information quickly and easily. The internet is also a good way of getting information.*

Part 2: Long turn

3 **Match pieces of advice 1–3 with reasons A–C.**

1 Remember the question is written above the photographs.

2 Don't try to give your own opinions during your partner's long turn.

3 Don't describe the pictures – you should compare them, then answer the question.

A This means you don't have to worry about forgetting what you have to talk about.

B The language you use when you describe is simple and you won't show how good you are.

C In this part of the test you both have to give an extended talk on your own.

4 **Look at the extract from a long turn below. Which piece of advice has the student forgotten?**

In the first picture I can see a man. He is wearing a red shirt and a hat. He is walking in front of a building which is quite tall and he is with a friend who is wearing a scarf. In the bottom corner I can see a tree which is also quite tall.

Part 3: Collaborative task

5 **Match pieces of advice 1–3 with reasons A–C.**

1 Respond to what your partner says and invite him/her to give his/her views.

2 Don't worry if you disagree with your partner, although you should be polite about this.

3 Say as much as you can about each option before you move on to the next.

A This gives you more to say on the topic and you will use more complex language.

B This often makes the discussion more interesting and lively.

C This is part of interactive communication, which is a communication skill.

6 **Look at the extract from a Part 3 discussion below. Which piece of advice have the students forgotten?**

A: *OK, we'll start with this prompt – working in an office.*

B: *That's not very interesting – what about studying hard?*

A: *I don't like that much. I prefer relaxing.*

B: *That's the third prompt. I like that, too.*

Part 4: Discussion

7 **Match pieces of advice 1–3 with reasons A–C.**

1 Listen to what your partner says and consider whether you think the same.

2 Try to give interesting reasons for your opinions and extend your answers.

3 Remember there are no right or wrong answers!

A The examiner just wants to hear you give your opinions in English.

B This is a real-life skill and gives you and your partner more to discuss.

C You may be asked whether you agree, so you must concentrate on your partner's ideas.

8 **Look at the question and answer from Part 4 given below. Which piece of advice has the student forgotten?**

A: *Why do people often choose to live in the country?*

B: *Fresh air, quiet, animals. It's good to live there.*

Practice test

Reading and Use of English

Part 1

For questions **1–8**, read the text below and decide which answer (**A**, **B**, **C** or **D**) best fits each gap. There is an example at the beginning (**0**).

Example

0 **A** in **B** at **C** under **D** with

Mark your answers **on the separate answer sheet**.

Making the most of your time

Nowadays we are all (**0**) _C, under_ pressure to increase the amount of work we can achieve in the shortest possible time. (**1**) .... of this we may spend time looking (**2**) .... short-cuts in our working lives. However, many of these time-saving measures may actually cause more problems than they (**3**) ....

Some organisations seem to expect their staff to work more than the usual eight or nine hours a day, without recognising the fact that tiredness causes people to (**4**) .... silly mistakes. We all tend to (**5**) .... those who can multi-task because we think they are working hard – but do all the electronic gadgets they use make them more efficient in the long (**6**) .... ? It's possible they actually distract them from the task (**7**) .... and lead to a loss of concentration. So maybe (**8**) .... every email or answering every mobile phone call immediately is not the most efficient use of our time.

1	**A** As a result	**B** Therefore	**C** Owing	**D** Due
2	**A** through	**B** out	**C** for	**D** in
3	**A** answer	**B** solve	**C** explain	**D** settle
4	**A** do	**B** get	**C** make	**D** have
5	**A** look up to	**B** get through to	**C** catch up with	**D** go out with
6	**A** walk	**B** run	**C** race	**D** hike
7	**A** in hand	**B** on hand	**C** by hand	**D** with hand
8	**A** A keeping in	**B** setting out	**C** taking on	**D** dealing with

Part 2

For questions **9–16**, read the text below and think of the word which best fits each gap. Use only one word in each gap. There is an example at the beginning (**0**).

Write your answers **IN CAPITAL LETTERS on the separate answer sheet**.

Example

0	F	O	R

Can you speak 'dog'?

We think we understand dogs, but we're often wrong about (**0**) _what_ they're trying to 'say'. Imagine trying to communicate (**9**) .... someone who doesn't understand any of your language. Dogs find (**10**) .... in this exact situation every day, and (**11**) .... are many examples of misunderstandings.

As (**12**) .... example of this, if a dog pants, we assume it's due to the heat. Of course, that may be true, but it could also indicate stress. (**13**) .... yawning might suggest tiredness, it could also signify an attempt to calm other dogs who are acting aggressively.

We think a dog wags its tail because it's happy, but there may be other meanings, depending (**14**) .... the position of the tail and the type of wag. (**15**) .... instance, when a dog holds its tail high and stiff, it's giving a warning. A dog does (**16**) .... if it thinks someone is trying to take its food, and may bite if the signal is ignored.

Clearly sometimes it's important to understand 'dog'!

Part 3

For questions **17–24**, read the text below. Use the word given in capitals at the end of some of the lines to form a word that fits in the gap **in the same line**. There is an example at the beginning (**0**).

Write your answers **IN CAPITAL LETTERS on the separate answer sheet**.

Example

0	D	I	F	F	E	R	E	N	C	E

Tourist or traveller?

People assume there is a (**0**) _difference_ between a tourist and a traveller and that 'tourist' is a negative term. Is this true?   **DIFFERENT**

In general, it seems a tourist goes to a new place to have a fun, (**17**) .... time, **ENJOY**
and to replace the energy used up by working in a (**18**) .... job. A traveller **STRESS**
wanders from place to place driven on by a deep (**19**) .... about everything **CURIOUS**
new and the desire to explore. A tourist escapes from the (**20**) .... routine **BORE**
of everyday life seeking relaxation, whereas all a traveller wants is to be on the road. A tourist goes somewhere, is amazed, but then returns with his or her everyday life
(**21**) .... by the experience; a traveller continues to roam around, seeking **CHANGE**
anything that enhances his or her (**22**) .... of the world. A tourist goes home **UNDERSTAND**
but a traveller moves on, perhaps unwilling to stop anywhere permanently.

But could it be possible that the two are (**23**) .... the same? After all, they **ACTUAL**
share a pleasure in the world and an (**24**) .... of the wonders in it. **APPRECIATE**

Part 4

For questions **25–30**, complete the second sentence so that it has a similar meaning to the first sentence, using the word given. **Do not change the word given.** You must use between two and five words, including the word given.

Here is an example (**0**).

Example

0   In class you have to do precisely what your teacher tells you.

CARRY

In class you have to .... instructions precisely.

The gap can be filled by 'carry out your teacher's', so you write:

Example

| **0** | *CARRY OUT YOUR TEACHER'S* |

Write your answers **IN CAPITAL LETTERS on the separate answer sheet.**

---

25   The moment I arrived at the hotel I checked my email.

SOON

I checked my email .... to the hotel.

26   They cancelled the meeting because the boss was ill.

OFF

The meeting .... the boss's illness.

27   I had never seen such an amazing waterfall before.

FIRST

It .... I had seen such an amazing waterfall.

28   It's a shame our school holidays are quite short in the summer.

WISH

I .... school holidays in the summer.

29   I always use my dictionary to check any words I'm not sure of.

UP

If I'm not sure of a word, ... my dictionary.

30   'You'd better hurry if you want to catch the bus, Joe,' said Juan.

ADVISED

Juan .... he would miss the bus.

You are going to read part of a magazine article about gorillas. For questions **31–36**, choose the answer (**A**, **B**, **C** or **D**) which you think fits best according to the text.

Mark your answers **on the separate answer sheet**.

How to see mountain gorillas

Back in 1979 when a TV film crew captured naturalist David Attenborough in a breathless encounter with mountain gorillas, such an experience seemed as improbable as walking with dinosaurs, and just as dangerous. Today we know better: we have nothing to fear from these gentle and highly endangered primates. And visiting them in their natural habitat – the mountain forests of equatorial Africa – has become one of the planet's ultimate wildlife experiences.

Scientifically speaking, the mountain gorilla is a high-altitude race of the eastern gorilla, the larger of Africa's two gorilla species, and distinguished by its denser fur, which protects it from the colder highlands climate. It lives in troops of 10–30 individuals, over which a 'silverback' male (named for his cape of white hair) presides. This formidable individual, sometimes topping 200kg, seldom uses his great strength in anger. Indeed, gorillas – compared with excitable chimps – are very relaxed animals.

Today the mountain gorilla is confined to a cluster of forested volcanoes that straddle the borders of Rwanda, Uganda and the Democratic Republic of Congo (DRC). It is much rarer than its lowland cousins further west but – thanks largely to American primatologist Diane Fossey – much better known. Fossey's work in Rwanda during the sixties and seventies radically changed our perception of these animals and, in the process, paved the way for today's tourist industry.

If you plan to go on a gorilla trek, your first requirement is a permit, which gets you one hour with the gorillas, plus the time it takes to hike there and back. Your trek is conducted under the supervision of park rangers. They will guide you to one of several habituated troops, whose movements are monitored around the
line 36 clock. Some may feel this makes the experience a little stage-managed. In reality, it is the only way to see wild gorillas. You cannot simply wander off by yourself: the terrain is too dangerous; the apes too elusive; and the rangers too focused on battling poachers to allow tourists to go it alone.

Treks set out daily. After an obligatory briefing, you will be assigned to a group of up to eight trekkers, plus guides and porters. Each group is allocated to a particular gorilla troop. The trek, including one hour with the gorillas, may take anything from three to nine hours, depending on the location of your troop. If you miss the briefing, or show up with a cold – which poses a serious health risk to the apes – you will be turned away, permit or no permit.

The dense undergrowth, high altitude and steep, slippery trail will soon have you scratched, muddy and exhausted. Tantalising clues along the way increase your excitement. But nothing prepares you for the intensity of the encounter. Many leave in tears, convinced that they've felt a 'connection'. While such ideas may be fanciful, there is no denying that sitting among the apes, meeting those searching, intelligent eyes in a face that seems to reflect your own, is a powerful experience.

Your guides will explain the rules. You should keep quiet and still and preserve a distance of seven metres – although there's nothing to stop the apes approaching you. Generally, nothing much happens: the gorillas are dozing or feeding, with some occasional rough and tumble among boisterous youngsters. The silverback is awesome to behold but nothing to worry about. If feeling tetchy, he may beat his chest or make a brief 'mock' charge. This sets the pulse racing but you need only keep still, avoid eye contact and let his bluster burn out. Your guides will be in control.

Gorilla trekking is, above all, an intimate experience which allows you the privilege of observing an extraordinary animal close-up. One hour is not enough, but it is an hour that you will remember for the rest of your life.

31 What, according to the writer, has changed since 1979 about our attitude to gorillas?

    A   We know they are an endangered species.

    B   We know where their habitats are located.

    C   We understand that they do not represent a threat.

    D   We believe that we are unlikely to encounter them in the wild.

32 What does the writer consider to be Diane Fossey's main contribution?

    A   She ensured that more people learnt about the mountain gorilla.

    B   She made it possible for people to visit the gorillas' habitats.

    C   She drew people's attention away from other types of gorilla.

    D   She made the mountain gorillas seem very lovable.

33 What does 'this' in line 36 refer to?

    A   The fact that you need a permit to visit the gorillas.

    B   The fact that the guides take you to where you are sure to see the gorillas.

    C   The fact that the gorillas' movements are tracked by the park authorities.

    D   The fact that you are only with the gorillas for an hour.

34 Under what circumstances would you be excluded from a trek?

    A   You refuse to go with the group to which you are assigned.

    B   You don't pay attention when the guides explain the rules.

    C   You are not willing to walk for so many hours.

    D   You have an illness that the gorillas could catch.

35 What does the writer think of people who say they feel 'a connection' with the gorillas?

    A   He thinks that they were not properly prepared for the experience.

    B   He feels sorry for them for getting so emotional.

    C   He thinks they are foolish for saying something like that.

    D   He understands why they might feel like that.

36 Why does the writer say the silver backs are 'nothing to worry about'?

    A   They only attack if people wake them up suddenly.

    B   They are only dangerous when they are young.

    C   They only make a show of being aggressive.

    D   They are intimidated by the guides.

Part 6

You are going to read an article about a woman who got lost while she was on holiday. Six sentences have been removed from the article. Choose from the sentences **A–G** the one which fits each gap (**37–42**). There is one extra sentence which you do not need to use.

Mark your answers **on the separate answer sheet**.

Lost in paradise

On my second trip to Greece I had a very embarrassing experience. I had arrived in Athens very early in the morning after a delayed flight from London on which I had barely slept a wink. My plan was to go to an island called Skopelos that a friend had recommended. It turned out that this involved a five-hour bus trip, at the end of which I had to catch a ferry to the island. By the time I got there, I had been travelling for over twenty-four hours.

As soon as the ferry docked at the little port, the other tourists and I were surrounded by local people offering us accommodation in their homes. I attached myself to a lovely woman called Nina and she led me up a winding path to her house, where she showed me to a pretty room with a private bathroom. | 37 | After getting dressed, I went down to the kitchen.

There, Nina was sitting with a young woman called Anika, who spoke Greek and English. While we had coffee, Anika acted as an interpreter. It turned out that Nina's daughter Olga was studying abroad, so Anika was staying in her room. Nina had suggested she should show me around the town. | 38 | We finished our coffee, said goodbye to Nina and headed out the door.

As we headed in the direction of the port, Anika pointed out various landmarks for me to remember: a house with a blue door and a lemon tree in a pot, a little chapel with a small bench outside, a café on a corner where there was a friendly little dog. | 39 | I wondered if I should go back to the house and have an early night but decided that I would be better off having something to eat before retracing my steps.

By the time Anika and I reached the port, it was time for her to go to work. | 40 | Although I was very hungry, I decided to make sure I could find my way back to Nina's while there was still some light.

From the port, I walked up a narrow path I could have sworn was the same one Nina and I had followed earlier that day. There was a café on a corner but no friendly dog, a little chapel but the bench was nowhere to be seen and there were several houses with blue doors and lemon trees. I had no idea where I was. | 41 | I began to wonder if Nina and her house were just a figment of my imagination.

Eventually, I realised that the simplest thing to do was to go back to the port and ask the tourist police to help me. | 42 | The police laughed when I told them that. It turned out that there were twenty women called Nina who rented out rooms and ten of them had daughters called Olga who were studying abroad.

The police were very kind, nevertheless, and telephoned every one of those women until on the tenth call they managed to find 'my Nina'. She came to get me and guided me back up to the house, chuckling to herself all the way. I collapsed into bed and slept for almost ten hours. The next day at breakfast I met an English couple who had had exactly the same experience.

A   I hadn't asked Nina to write down her address but at least I knew her name.

B   This meant that I was on my own, and the sun was beginning to set.

C   The harder I tried to remember exactly what Anika had said, the more lost I became.

D   Since it was late June, it would still be light for a couple of hours.

E   I had a much needed shower and unpacked.

F   Surely he would know where Nina lived.

G   I tried to pay attention but my tiredness made it difficult to take it all in.

Part 7

You are going to read some information about five musicians and the instruments they play. For questions **43–52**, choose from the musicians (**A–E**). The musicians may be chosen more than once.

Mark your answers **on the separate answer sheet**.

Which musician

was inspired by seeing someone perform?	43
feels the instrument suits their personality?	44
stopped playing the instrument at one stage?	45
says the instrument suits them physically?	46
feels their instrument is sometimes a nuisance?	47
had not seriously considered playing this instrument at first?	48
did not make the decision to play an instrument?	49
did not find it difficult to learn the basics?	50
travels frequently?	51
plays an instrument previously owned by someone else?	52

Heart strings

A   The guitarist

My father played the guitar and the banjo and had learnt both from my grandfather. All my uncles played too. By the time I came along, it was a well-established family tradition. There was just no question about whether I would learn to play an instrument or not and what instrument that would be. I got my first guitar when I was seven. My father bought me a second-hand instrument because they are easier to play and tune. Since that time, I have owned more than twenty guitars. I've sold some of them, lost one and had two stolen, but I've always managed to hang on to that original guitar. I've played it often and looked after it carefully over the years, so it is still in quite good condition.

B   The mandolin player

My mother came home from work one evening with a mandolin. I already knew how to play the guitar so it didn't take me long to work out how to play a few chords. I strummed it from time to time, showed it to all my friends and then stuck it behind the sofa where it stayed for several years. In my second term at college, my parents phoned to say they were planning to come and visit me and asked me if there was anything in particular I would like them to bring from home. I don't know why but suddenly I realised I badly wanted the mandolin. So they brought it with them and I've never looked back.

C   The double bass player

Children didn't normally learn the double bass in the past. The instruments were just too big for tiny fingers and little arms. As a result, most of my friends who play started with the violin but my teacher managed to get me an instrument specially designed for children. It was a tenth the

normal size and very cute. Size is always a problem though. We play abroad quite a lot and getting my instrument through security is a real headache. Even getting round town is not easy. Despite all the inconvenience, I love my bass. It's a perfect instrument for someone like me who is rather shy and not really interested in being centre stage. I'd much rather make music with other people.

D   The harp player

My parents took me to a concert but from where we were sitting, I couldn't see the strings of the harp. I just saw the hands move through the air and heard these beautiful sounds that took me into another world. Much later, when I started to play myself, I realised that because of the way you sit behind the harp and take its weight on your shoulders, you feel every sound as a vibration that passes through your body. It's wonderful. Unfortunately, not all concert music includes a part for the harp, so you don't have as many opportunities to play with others as some musicians do. I think that's a great pity.

E   The viola player

A lot of people don't even know the difference between a viola and a cello. They just know that they're not violins. I was a bit the same when I was younger because my father was a concert violinist and he really didn't take the viola seriously. I played the violin too. When I was studying violin at university I attended a chamber music class with a famous professor. He took a viola out of its case and said, 'You will play the viola.' I was very reluctant even to touch it but I have fairly long arms and the violin had always been a bit uncomfortable for me. The viola felt much less cramped. I played the first note and said to myself, 'My goodness, this is fun!'

Writing

Part 1

You **must** answer this question. Write your answer in **140–190** words in an appropriate style.

In your English class you have been talking about the advantages and disadvantages of buying things online instead of in person in a shop. Now, your English teacher has asked you to write an essay.

Write an essay using **all** the notes and give reasons for your point of view.

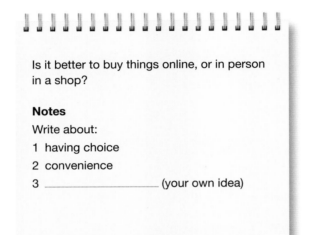

Is it better to buy things online, or in person in a shop?

Notes

Write about:

1 having choice

2 convenience

3 _____ (your own idea)

Part 2

Write an answer to **one** of the questions **2–4** in this part. Write your answer in **140–190** words in an appropriate style.

2   The principal wants to extend the type of activities students can do after school, and has asked for suggestions. Write a report for the principal outlining the current situation, explaining any problems there are and recommending changes, with reasons.

Write your **report**.

3   You have seen this announcement in an international film magazine.

Film reviews wanted!

We're asking readers to send in a review of the best or worst film they have ever seen. We will publish the most interesting reviews!

Write your **review**.

4   You have received an email from your Portuguese friend, Jose.

Hi!

I'm planning to visit your country in July. I'd like to spend a short time seeing the most important sights and then I want to find a part-time job for a few weeks to help me learn the language.

Can you give me some advice on what to see, and the kind of part-time work I could get? Is it easy to find work?

Many thanks,

Jose

Write your **email**.

Listening

Part 1 ▶ 25

You will hear people talking in eight different situations. For questions **1–8**, choose the best answer (**A**, **B** or **C**).

1 You overhear a woman leaving a voicemail message on a theatre answerphone.
  What does she want to do?
  A get her money back
  B go to a different performance
  C change her seats for better ones

2 You hear two people talking about a film they have just seen.
  What do they agree about?
  A The advertising for the film was misleading.
  B The acting was unusually effective.
  C The special effects were unmemorable.

3 You overhear two people talking at an airport.
  The man is annoyed because
  A he doesn't want to miss his meeting.
  B he doesn't like flying with a particular airline.
  C he doesn't understand why the flight is delayed.

4 You overhear a woman on the phone talking about her course at college.
  What does she think about the course?
  A It is more difficult than she'd expected.
  B It is less interesting than she'd previously hoped.
  C It is more time-consuming than she'd anticipated.

5 You hear two people talking about a type of television programme called a game show.
  What do they agree about game shows?
  A They have become ridiculous.
  B They are rarely cost-effective.
  C They can sometimes be quite amusing.

6 You hear a young singer talking on a radio chat show.
  How does he feel about his latest career move?
  A disappointed not to be doing better
  B upset by people's attitude towards him
  C sorry that he can't sing the kind of songs he likes

7 You hear a woman talking on the radio about chewing gum.
  What is she doing?
  A outlining the history of the product
  B highlighting problems with the product
  C explaining the popularity of the product

8 You hear part of a phone-in programme on the radio.
  Why has the man phoned?
  A to suggest a way of improving the programme
  B to complain about the attitude of other listeners
  C to criticise the way the presenter deals with different topics

Part 2 ▶ 26

You hear a woman called Anne Roberts talking to a group of students about doing a job called a runner in the film industry. For questions **9–18**, complete the sentences with a word or short phrase.

Working as a runner in the film industry

Anne says that her ambition is to be a **(9)** .... of films.

Anne uses the words **(10)** .... to describe the kind of work she does as a runner.

Anne found it peculiar that she did a lot of **(11)** .... on her first job as a runner.

Anne thought it was funny when she had to collect some **(12)** .... that had been forgotten.

Anne found working with the **(13)** .... very helpful.

Anne says being what she refers to as a good **(14)** .... is crucial.

According to Anne, having good **(15)** .... is very important for a runner.

Anne says it is difficult finding work through **(16)** ....

According to Anne, people become runners because they hope to establish useful **(17)** .... in the film industry.

What Anne likes most about working in films is the atmosphere of **(18)** .... on the set.

Part 3 27

You will hear five different people talking about being a good presenter. For questions **19–23**, choose from the list (**A–H**) what each speaker thinks is most important for a good presenter. Use the letters only once. There are three extra letters which you do not need to use.

A	including specialist vocabulary	Speaker 1	19
B	telling amusing anecdotes	Speaker 2	20
C	speaking loudly and clearly	Speaker 3	21
D	being completely honest	Speaker 4	22
E	keeping good eye contact	Speaker 5	23
F	using appropriate body language		
G	handling technology well		
H	adapting to the audience		

Part 4 28

You will hear an interview with Kris Ashton, a successful young tennis player. For questions **24–30**, choose the best answer (**A**, **B** or **C**).

24 How did Kris feel about tennis when he was young?

    A   upset because he preferred a different sport

    B   frustrated because he couldn't practise with friends

    C   annoyed because his parents forced him to play tennis

25 What is Kris's attitude now to his experiences at school?

    A   He accepts that it was important to study.

    B   He is glad that it showed him how to be successful.

    C   He appreciates the opportunity he had to make lasting friendships.

26 What does Kris say about his early competitive years?

    A   It was fortunate that older players accepted him.

    B   He had to grow up more quickly than other people.

    C   It would have been better to have spent more time at college.

27 What does Kris say about his exercise routine and diet?

    A   He finds it difficult to eat healthy meals.

    B   He resents the need for strict discipline.

    C   He understands that his training has to be varied.

28 What does Kris enjoy most about being a tennis professional?

    A   travelling round the world

    B   making a lot of money

    C   meeting new people

29 What advice would Kris give to young players?

    A   Enjoy yourself as much as you can.

    B   Listen to people who know more than you.

    C   Try to achieve your ambitions as quickly as possible.

30 What ambitions does Kris have for the future?

    A   to help younger players achieve their potential

    B   to be successful in another sport

    C   to work in the media

Speaking

Part 1

The Interlocutor will ask you and the other candidate some questions about yourselves.

▶ 29 Listen to the recording and answer the questions. Pause the recording after each bleep and give your answer.

Part 2

The Interlocutor will ask you and the other candidate to talk on your own about some photographs.

▶ 30 Listen to the recording and answer the questions. When you hear two bleeps, answer the question. You have one minute. When you hear one bleep, answer the second question. You have 30 seconds.

Candidate A

What do you think the people are enjoying about learning to do these different things?

Candidate B

Why is this moment important to the people?

Part 3

The Interlocutor will ask you and the other candidate to discuss something together.

▶ 31 Look at the task and listen to the Interlocutor's instructions. When you hear the bleep, discuss the task. You have two minutes.

Listen to the Interlocutor's instructions. When you hear the bleep, discuss and make your decision. You have one minute.

Part 4

The Interlocutor will ask you and the other candidate questions related to the topic of Part 3.

▶ 32 Listen to the recording and answer the interlocutor's questions. Pause the recording when you hear each bleep and discuss the question with the other candidate.

Audio scripts

Unit 1, Speaking Activity 1

Track 01

1 What kind of music do you enjoy listening to?
2 Do you have any brothers or sisters?
3 What do you like about the place where you were brought up?
4 What subject did you like most at school?
5 What do you think you'll be doing in five years' time?
6 Where do you think you'll go on holiday this year?
7 Who is your closest friend?

Unit 1, Listening Activity 1

Track 02

Speaker 1: I hadn't really got any particular expectations before I went, even though it was my first time – obviously my friends had told me about the last gig they went to, but nothing really prepared me for the sheer size of the venue. The stage was well lit but we were so far away from it that it might as well have been somewhere else. I did quite like the music, though I could have been listening on an MP3 player. And the cost of getting in seemed rather unfair – it wasn't very good value for money, given how little I could see.

Speaker 2: It was the band that attracted me to go in the first place – I love their music, and I've bought all their albums – and the cost of the gig seemed pretty reasonable. I went with three mates, and we had a good time watching the rest of the people and eating the food and drink that you could buy from loads of stalls around the site. The stage wasn't that great, and the view was pretty rubbish – but what really got me was what I'd actually gone for – the music was distorted and I couldn't hear it properly. My mates said the same thing.

Speaker 3: I've always liked the band, and have been to some of their concerts before so I thought I knew what to expect. I knew that the cost would be ridiculously high, the food would be expensive and poor and that the only way to see them properly would be to watch the big screens on either side of the stage – though one of my mates was really put out about that! It was what they chose to perform that I was less keen on – instead of doing their hits they tried this new experimental stuff. Not my thing at all, and I nearly left early.

Speaker 4: I really love listening to any live music, whatever it is – for me the whole experience is really improved by actually being there and sharing it with all the others. That's why I found this concert such a let-down – there was no atmosphere and instead of getting up and dancing everyone just sat watching the band on stage.

Maybe they didn't like the music – I agree that it wasn't up to their normal standards – but if you make the effort to go to these things then at least join in! The place itself was impressive, though.

Speaker 5: I know that most people think that the only important thing is the music – and of course that's pretty important! But when I go out for the evening, I expect to have a good all-round experience, especially when the tickets are pretty pricey! This concert was let down not by the music, which I thought was cool, but the place itself. OK, I could see the stage and there was a good atmosphere generally, but trying to get anything to eat was ridiculous – the queues were so long that you missed loads of music. And don't even get me started on the wait for the toilets.

Unit 2, Listening Activity 1

Track 03

Interviewer: Susie – you're only fourteen and you're already singing and dancing in a successful musical. How have your family reacted, and how do you feel about that?

Susie: Well, my parents both sang and danced when they were young, and we used to have musical evenings at home. I guess some people might think it's in my genes, though I'm not sure! I'm quite close to both my sisters, though their interest is sport. Organising us all was a tough balancing act for my parents, but luckily they always managed to be there for me. I'm not sure they realised how serious I was, though.

Interviewer: How did you get on with students at your first school?

Susie: It was a normal school. The students there were jealous and teased me a lot, but I was so focused, it just washed over me. I always got the main part in any school entertainment, which I realised was what made them resent me so much. Once I'd transferred to a vocational theatre school, everyone had the same mindset. The downside was the competitive environment, which was hard to adjust to – I was used to being the best.

Interviewer: How do you feel about getting into a stage production so young?

Susie: There are three of us sharing the role – I don't perform every night – so it's not as tough as you might think. Some supporters come to the stage door after a show, which I don't mind, but talking to them can be quite time-consuming. For me the real buzz is when I'm actually on the stage. My favourite part is taking the bows – that probably sounds big-headed but it's great to know the audience have enjoyed the show and I've made them happy. I'm emotionally shattered after a performance, though that passes when I get back to school.

Interviewer: How do you get on with the adult performers?

Susie: I don't hang out with them much, but they've really helped me with the technical stuff like being in the right place on stage. In the early days rehearsals were pretty difficult as the director is a real perfectionist, and everything had to be exactly right. I was hopeless at projecting my voice, but I'm more confident about that now.

Interviewer: Who's your best friend and why is that relationship important to you?

Susie: It used to be my sister, but now we're not so close. I have a school friend, Jake – he shares my dreams, so I can talk to him and he just gets it. He's a bit older and has been in several stage productions, so I value what he says cos it comes from experience. He's very sensible and doesn't make me feel bad if I want to express my concerns or worries.

Interviewer: Do you regret anything about your career choices so far?

Susie: There are sacrifices – like I don't see much of my sisters and I haven't hung out with my friends for ages, but that's part and parcel of the path I've chosen. Sometimes I think it'd be nice to be like everyone else because I have to be ready to go on even when I'm not scheduled in case the other girl is ill, or gets injured at the last minute. Critics can be harsh in their reviews, but I try not to take any notice of them. Life's a compromise for everyone, isn't it?

Interviewer: The musical's won lots of awards – how do you feel about that?

Susie: I guess it's overwhelming and motivating at the same time. Getting one has given me a deep sense of responsibility – a feeling that I have to make the most of my talent, which is stressful. Obviously it's nice to be part of a production that's considered outstanding, but I don't do it for the glamour or recognition – being on stage is a privilege, and I'm aware that not everyone has the opportunities I've had.

Interviewer: Thanks, Susie – and good luck with the show!

Unit 2, Speaking Activity 1
Track 04

1

Woman: I think it's so important to get on well with your parents.

Man: So do I. I have a great relationship with my folks. I think it's more important than getting on with your brothers and sisters.

Woman: Hmm. I'm not sure about that. I mean, I think it's important to have a good relationship with them too.

Man: It's much more difficult if you come from a very large family.

Woman: I hadn't thought of that. I guess it's almost inevitable that there will be someone you don't get along so well with if there are a lot of you.

Man: Exactly! There are five of us and though I get on fine with my older brother and with my two sisters, my younger brother and I just don't have anything in common. What about you?

Woman: Well, I've only got one sister and I really enjoy doing things with her.

2

Woman 1: I saw a programme about relationships last night that said that friends were more important than family.

Woman 2: I saw it too – but I'm not convinced. Certainly friends are pretty crucial – it'd be a poor social life without them! But family must always come first.

Woman 1: I see what you mean but some things the programme said are certainly true for me. They said your friends have a lot more influence on you when you're young than your parents do. What's your view on that?

Woman 2: Well, actually in my case it was the other way round. I learnt my values from my parents. I think it's their responsibility to teach you how to behave.

Woman 1: Good point. Parents do need to teach their children how to behave but I think you can also learn from your friends.

Unit 3, Listening Activity 1
Track 05

Hi, everyone – it's great to be here and have the chance to share with you what I do and why I feel it's so important. I've been passionate about animals and the environment all my life – to me it's what matters most. Although it was quite near a town, I actually grew up on a small farm, so I was always surrounded by animals – all sorts of different things – ducks, chickens, horses – I used to milk the goats before I went to school every morning and collect the eggs when I got home – I loved that. But as I got older, I realised how other people aren't lucky enough to have this closeness to nature – particularly children brought up in cities who don't really see animals in their natural state.

I also love adventure – my favourite leisure activities include going rock-climbing and hiking – and once I started travelling round the world to remote places like rainforests and deserts I got completely hooked on the plight of endangered animals and ways of trying to save them. When I got the chance to audition as the presenter on a new children's television programme about dangerous animals, I jumped at it. Although you may think it's glamorous I think the best way for me to describe it is tough, though I love to be out there in the natural world.

What makes it so perfect? What's crucial for me is that although we show lots of dangerous animals which engages the children's interest, the strong message that runs through every programme is conservation.

A large proportion of the animals we film are on the endangered list and we've done 'endangered animal' special programmes as well. It's my responsibility to present the wider picture that goes beyond just showing off a dangerous animal for the thrill of it.

The most important thing for me is that the programme speaks to young people – they're the future, and if we can save species under threat, then it's the children who'll do it. What I want is to give them a sense of involvement with my programme in ways they'll remember and that will affect their future thinking. Children want to know what it's really like to be with me in the Arctic or in the jungle.

When we're filming, we never know what's around the corner. It isn't scripted, so if I suddenly come across a giant snake, the film crew can capture my shock. Over the years I've been charged by an elephant, followed by a tiger – and the cameras were there last year when I tripped over a crocodile in swampland and needed hospital treatment! The children loved that!

How important is my work? I can't emphasise enough that TV does a remarkable job of bringing the major issues to light. It's made children more aware of things like climate change and how that affects wildlife. It's great watching them when they come across an animal they've never seen before. They're inspired and totally in awe.

I do know not everyone agrees with me – sociologists have argued that children's lives are becoming even more disconnected from the natural world because they're increasingly immersed in technology. How we go about changing this and reconnecting young people with the natural world is a challenge, and one I'm proud to take on.

However, if the success of my own programme is anything to go by, sociologists haven't got it completely right. Expeditions to the world's most remote places are still the most exciting thing for me – I've been inside a volcano, and found new species in jungles, such as the world's largest rat! But, I don't just show what's there – what's so important to me is to search for a way to save the places I explore. I can't bear the thought of being in this world without trying to do something to look after it – that's what matters to me. So, does anyone have any questions?

Unit 3, Speaking Activity I

Track 06

Examiner: I'm going to give each of you two photographs. Carla, here are your photographs. I'd like you to compare the photographs and say how you think the people are feeling. You have about a minute to do this.

Carla: These photographs are similar because they both show groups of people but they are very different in other ways. The first photograph shows people on a beach, whereas the people in the second photograph are probably in a city or town as they are in some kind of sports stadium. In the first photograph, the people look like they care about the environment because they are cleaning the beach, and they are working hard although on the other hand the people in the second photograph

look more relaxed because it seems as though the football team has won a trophy. They all look happy. The people on the beach look as if they are upset about the condition of the beach although they must be pleased to be doing something about it, and there are also children helping.

Unit 4, Listening Activity I

Track 07

Interviewer: Today in our series of incredible exploits we're talking to Alan Preston, a young man who sailed round the world alone at the age of sixteen. Alan, what were you like as a child?

Alan: My parents say I was born adventurous, and I love outdoor life. We spent our family holidays going camping, hiking, things like that – I was always ready to have a go at anything I hadn't done before. Once we went out in a small boat exploring. I loved it, and although my sister wasn't keen, that experience was the defining moment for me. I started reading about sailors and, although I was still fascinated by all kinds of adventure sports, it was sailing that had the edge. Dad encouraged me – he'd been in the navy and I think he hoped I'd follow him in that.

Interviewer: How did you start taking sailing seriously?

Alan: Dad had always wanted to sail across the Atlantic single-handed, but mum discouraged him because she was worried. But he and I talked about it, and as I got better at sailing, it kind of took on its own momentum. I was fourteen when I did it – but dad followed me in a back-up boat to make sure I was all right. After that the sailing bug really took hold – I felt like I had a purpose in life. Although I still did teenage things, I had a kind of inner strength. I knew what I wanted to do.

Interviewer: What made you decide to sail round the world?

Alan: I was sixteen when I started planning and I had to get money somehow – dad and I had to raise sponsorship. Some people criticised my parents for being pushy but they were just supportive. I'd never have left port unless I was committed to the challenge and knew I was capable. But I was lucky to be allowed to do it, given the dangers! I actually left the final decision to mum who said making it was almost impossible, but in the end she went along with dad and me.

Interviewer: How did it feel when you started out on such a long trip?

Alan: There's a gap between imagining something and doing it! Those first days were the hardest, 'cos there were loads of technical problems which got me down – I even thought I might have to give up! That would've been disappointing, but I carried on, sleeping in periods of 20–40 minutes, eating rehydrated meals – some people said I'd be lonely, but my mates had put loads of music on my iPod which was great. I'd stuck photos everywhere and packed loads of clothes so I didn't need to worry about doing any washing!

Interviewer: What was the worst moment?

Alan: I love the roller-coaster ride of huge seas – I was in tune with the boat, surfing down fifty-foot waves. I felt confident I could cope. But there was this one storm that I knew was forecast – it had massive waves and the boat turned over on its side. The damage meant I had to climb to the top of the seventy-foot mast to repair it in terrible winds – the only time I wore body armour and a helmet for protection! That was pretty scary – I was glad to get back to the cabin!

Interviewer: Why do you keep sailing?

Alan: It's the feeling of being completely in control and in tune with natural forces. I've had dolphins swimming alongside, seen stunning, vivid sunsets. It's those kinds of moments when it feels like the world stops and you believe anything is possible. It's not the racing against other people, though I'm proud to be doing it so young – I don't bother much about records and stuff.

Interviewer: What advice would you give young people about taking on this kind of challenge?

Alan: One thing is to be ready mentally for anything – sometimes during the voyage, I'd think, why am I here, this is awful. Then I'd remember mum and dad and what it would be like at the finish. That got me through. Listen to any advice you're given but decide for yourself, though probably the most crucial thing is, don't lose sight of what's real – I still have sailing ambitions but for now, it's back to ordinary life – I've got to go back to college to finish my exams.

Unit 4, Speaking Activity 1

Track 08

A: OK. Let's talk about taking risks. In my opinion, no one should put themselves in danger.

B: I don't agree – I think that young people can become much more confident if they manage to do difficult things, especially on their own.

A: That's true, but not everyone is brave like that, and it may actually have the opposite effect and make them less confident.

B: OK. I accept that, but it's always a good idea for young people to get new experiences.

A: You're right – and it's difficult for anyone to do that if they never take any risks at all.

B: Plus, don't forget that it can be fun! You don't know about that unless you try.

Unit 5, Listening Activity 2

Track 09

Hi, everyone – I'm Terri and I'm here to talk about my job, which is one that many of you may never have heard of! I'm sure you've had experiences of diets of different kinds – well, I'm a nutritionist – but not for people, for horses. How did that come about? My childhood loves were animals and science, and my parents always imagined I'd be a vet – I did think about it, and also about studying medicine, but in the end I did a biology degree at university which was when I got interested in food and health in general. I then discovered that there was a module in animal nutrition – and everything took off from there. I now work in a department involved in research into the physical state of horses and what makes them fat, so I can advise horse breeders and owners on the best diet for the animals to follow. I've recently been involved in a study on how much grass horses eat compared with other food. During this trial, it was found that some horses ate up to five to seven percent of their own bodyweight in grass daily – which amounts to an extra weight gain of approximately three kilograms a day on average. We used to think that horses ate around sixty-two kilos of the stuff in a day – however we now know that it's double this and is actually around a hundred and twenty-five kilograms every single day – incredible! My work is pretty varied on a day-to-day basis – yesterday I spent the day out with a vet weighing and measuring a selection of horses. They were all pretty big so I spent most of my day standing on my toes and I ache all over now! I'm not always out with the animals – I also spend a lot of time in the office having meetings and also doing paperwork – not my favourite occupation! We have a telephone helpline where people can call with questions or problems, and although some might find it challenging as you get put on the spot by callers, for me it's very rewarding. As with any job there are highs and lows. I'm trying to get a message across – what makes horses fat – and work out how to educate people – it's a bit like dealing with human diets really. Once people understand, they are desperate to change things, but I have to work out ways of raising that awareness. I also get irritated that I have to rely on others for the money that enables me to do my work – we're not funded. I'm actually still very interested in human nutrition – and now there is a massive demand for it – it's big business. I have to stay up to date with all the latest developments. My approach to any kind of diet though is the same – people often try to cut down on everything, but for me moderation is the key. I don't think anyone has to avoid eating bad things, but if you eat them you have to make compromises elsewhere – for example, if you have a chocolate bar, cut down on the toast! The main reason why both humans and horses put on weight is lack of exercise but you can't treat them the same. You have to treat horses like horses not people – and they need proper exercise. The industry as a whole needs a bit of a shake-up. We seem to be at two ends of extremes – on the one hand we have ground-breaking science in the form of veterinary research such as stem cell treatments, but on the other people are still not open-minded to new approaches and tend to stick to what they know. But the great thing is that everyone who works with horses is passionate about them.

Unit 5, Speaking Activity 1

Track 10

Your photographs show people eating in different places. I'd like you to compare the photographs and say what you think the people are enjoying about eating in these places.

Unit 5, Speaking Activity 3

Track 11

I think we all like joining our friends and family for meals like those we see in the photos. It's particularly enjoyable to eat in the open air but even an ordinary meal like breakfast in the kitchen is a good time for the family to get together and talk before the beginning of a busy working day or at the weekends when there's a bit more time.

Unit 6, Speaking Activity 1

Track 12

1

Interlocutor: Ana, what do you think would be hardest about being a famous actor or musician – the lack of privacy or the need to constantly compete with others?

Ana: Definitely the lack of privacy. I think it must be very difficult to be constantly surrounded by paparazzi and journalists watching everything you do. And often it's not just the actor or musician; it's their whole family. Competition is healthy in some ways because it makes us perform at our best, but never having a moment to yourself must be almost unbearable. Would you agree with that, Mario?

Mario: No. I think it would be good to be famous.

Ana: Well, I suppose you're right up to a point. The money would obviously be very useful and it would be great to feel that you had achieved something important but I still think that often the media are just waiting for the star to make some kind of mistake and then it's all over the front page of the newspapers.

2

Interlocutor: Celina, what do you think of international competitions like the Eurovision Song Contest?

Celina: I think they're great. It's like a huge party with young people from literally all over Europe taking part. We get to hear great pop music in all the European languages and see Europe's best young artists performing live.

Interlocutor: What do you think, Gabriel?

Gabriel: Like you, Celina, I'm a big fan of the Eurovision Song Contest. I never miss it. What you're saying is that it offers us the very best of European pop music. I'm not sure about that. I mean, not all the acts are of equally high quality and sometimes the artists themselves are not really representative of the best their countries have to offer.

Unit 6, Listening Activity 1

Track 13

Extract 1

M: I just loved it – the music was brilliant!

F: I'm gutted that it was their last show together. Did you read in the programme that they've recorded it and are going to put it out on DVD – ah, it'll be great to see it again, though it probably won't be the same as it was tonight. No atmosphere.

M: It'll be interesting when the lead singer goes into the theatre as he says he will – he's talented enough on the singing front, but what about the acting and dancing?

F: Well, we'll have to give him a chance. I'll certainly go and see him, especially after tonight!

Extract 2

M: How did I start? Well, I'd never imagined that I'd actually be a teacher – that's what both my parents did and my grandparents as well, though they never pressured me into doing it. I was around sixteen when I really became interested in science and mechanical engineering, and so the idea of working in a college rather than a school seemed on the cards. I suppose I could say that I kind of stumbled into it, but I've been doing it for three years now and I can't say I've ever regretted the decision. It wasn't a particularly cool thing to do according to my mates, of course!

Extract 3

F: I'd really like to go home and see if it's OK.

M: But you always turn it off – it's just an automatic reaction. Don't be silly!

F: It's just that I can't remember doing it – I know you always laugh if I say that but you don't understand how it feels!

M: Well, I haven't got time to go back with you now – I've got a meeting in half an hour – and the bus is coming. If you want to, then I'll have to go ahead and catch up with you at lunchtime.

F: Maybe that's the best thing to do.

Extract 4

M: Thanks for finally having me on – I've been waiting ages! At least I can have my say now. I've been listening for the last hour and I can't believe what your callers are saying. They must know whatever anyone does on the recycling front – big or small – makes a difference. We're all responsible for the world we live in – how can they moan about being asked to put rubbish in different bins? But I accept that not everyone sees it like that, so I think we should be given incentives to do it – that would get people on side, and be pretty easy to put into operation I'd have thought.

Extract 5

M: During my research for this programme – which was originally going to be concentrating on finding new and different forms of heating and so on – it became clear that we're just not doing enough to look after the planet in general terms – recycling, that sort of thing. I realise it's not easy, but I was taken aback by how little the average person in the street seemed to know or think about it – so that caused a shift of emphasis. I now see it as a wake-up call, bringing the kinds of things we can all do out into the open.

Extract 6

F: Well, that was pretty much a waste of time – after those fantastic reviews I'd had high hopes!

M: I'd been told that it was disappointing, so I was kind of prepared. But I hadn't thought that the actors would be so off – she's usually brilliant.

F: And he doesn't often put in a bad performance – pity it was this film! At least the technology didn't let anyone down – the flying scenes were spectacular.

M: But they didn't do anything really cutting edge, did they? I mean I've seen it all before.

F: They had me on the edge of my seat!

Extract 7

M: Did the meeting go OK?

F: I guess. When I presented the policy plan it seemed to go down well. Even the technology worked, which I had nightmares about because I knew the big bosses would be there! The question and answer session afterwards went well – the time I spent preparing paid off.

M: You said the kids got fed up with you working in the evenings so at least now you can spend some time with them.

F: Well, I've still got to write up the report – it'll be circulated next week. I haven't told my husband yet but next weekend will be busy!

M: I'll see it soon then.

Extract 8

F: We've been friends for a long time and it'd be a pity if we can't disagree on some things and still stay friends. You know that I don't think that what you're saying is right and it's difficult to go along with you when you say things like that – but we need to move on from the whole incident, OK? I may be wrong and you may be proved right in the end – but just now I think we must change the subject before we actually come to blows over it. That would be a big mistake!

Unit 7, Speaking Activity 1

Track 14

Here are your two photographs. They show people celebrating their wedding in different situations. I'd like you to compare the photographs, and say why you think people have chosen to celebrate their weddings in these situations.

Unit 7, Speaking Activity 3

Track 15

Well, the first couple have chosen to have a cycling wedding. I imagine they are on their way to the reception in the photograph and that the wedding ceremony itself must have already taken place. They seem to be very happy about it, and the other members of the wedding party look as if they are enjoying it too. The other couple have decided to have one of their wedding photos taken under water. They can't have had the actual wedding there. I'm absolutely certain of that. The first couple are definitely cycling fanatics. They must really love the sport if they have chosen to cycle to the reception. The other couple could have just wanted an unusual wedding photograph for their wedding album. I suppose an underwater photograph would be rather difficult to take but it might be fun. As far as I can see there's nobody else in the photo, so I'm fairly certain it was also taken after the wedding itself. It might even have been taken the day after. It wouldn't be much fun sitting through the reception in a wet wedding dress!

Unit 7, Listening Activity 2

Track 16

Interviewer: Today we're talking to Karen Wilson, a talented musician and photographer who produces unusual, thought-provoking travel books. Karen, how did you start?

Karen: My home town was very traditional and I wasn't outstanding at school. I was persuaded to take up the classical guitar and learn music theory, but then I studied piano and drums – it was those classes that I found most engaging, and I thought it would be my only career. But I was always good at drawing – visual stuff appealed to me, though teachers didn't push me. Photography wasn't on the syllabus, and it was never suggested as a realistic career option.

Interviewer: How did you get started as a photographer?

Karen: I'd been taking photographs for years as a hobby, though I didn't really show them to many other people at the time. I loved photographing unusual things – empty places like airport buildings, theatres – stuff like that. I was travelling a lot for my music, and putting photographs I took during tours on a website. By chance a publisher saw them and asked me to write a book combining photographs with a travel diary. I couldn't turn down that opportunity to express myself and it all took off after that.

Interviewer: How do you approach your books?

Karen: I heard something in an interview that was a great influence on me – a photo-journalist said that photographers were privileged people who should record things other people don't get the chance to see – that it's our responsibility to open people's eyes to things they wouldn't otherwise be aware of. Most people think travel is always exciting and positive. I want to show the strangeness of it – make people realise it's not always glamorous, especially when you're doing it for work as I do.

Interviewer: What do you find fascinating about different places?

Karen: You think every big city is beautiful – and of course they are. But when I'm touring I have to go to parts of cities that aren't – like backstage in large venues outside the main tourist areas. It's weird – I read travel guides or look down at a city from a plane as it's coming in to land and it looks wonderful – but then I go to a characterless hotel room or desolate rehearsal space and it's not the same at all. I've talked to people about this contradiction, but they don't feel it like I do.

Interviewer: Tell us about a trip that you really enjoyed.

Karen: That would be when I went to the south of Argentina. Its beauty comes from a kind of stillness, a grandeur that's based on its landscape and wildlife. I did a few gigs at the start of the trip, which all went really well, then took time off and rented a car to drive along parts of the coastline. I hardly saw anyone – just birds and miles of remote countryside. It was so different from New York – you can't get away from people there.

Interviewer: What have you learnt from your travel experiences?

Karen: Ah, before I became a touring musician I did loads of travelling with the family, but we only scratched the surface of places we visited. It was ticking boxes – been there, done that. Of course I still enjoy that part of it – some places are so remarkable you can't not enjoy them. But now I try to get beneath the surface, listen to the sounds and soak in the atmosphere. That's where photography comes in for me – it makes me concentrate on a single image which helps me comprehend much more about a place.

Interviewer: What do you think has made you so successful?

Karen: Well, I've been so fortunate to combine music and photography – clearly if you love what you do, it helps! I've also had lots of support both personally and professionally, though that's just a bonus really. For me it's about not accepting the obvious but searching for things that lie deeper. If you push boundaries, you enrich yourself personally – and that's really what I think has been the key!

Interviewer: Thank you, Karen – and good luck with the next tour!

Unit 8, Listening Activity 2

Track 17

Speaker 1: I got interested in the whole area of sport when I started school, though I loved playing with a ball from a very early age. My parents always encouraged me, though I think they regarded it as a hobby rather than an actual career – we didn't know what the opportunities were then. I went on adventure holidays where sporting activities were top of my list, but it wasn't until I talked to a careers adviser that I realised how many possibilities sport offered apart from playing and, more importantly, how much money I could earn! That's when I decided I'd become a personal trainer.

Speaker 2: I come from a family of teachers – in that kind of environment there's always an expectation you'll

automatically do the same thing. I've always known it wasn't for me, but I also knew they'd be disappointed – that was hard. But since I was young I've had this desire to be a dancer, though I know it's a very difficult life. I've taken the first steps towards achieving my ambition in that I'm at a vocational school, but whether I'll ever be good enough to earn big money like the stars, travelling all over the world, I have no idea. But if I don't try, I'll never know.

Speaker 3: I'd always intended to do something related to my main interest, which is music – my parents have always encouraged me to play various instruments since I was very young – we used to play music together as a family – and I can't imagine my life without it. Once I started looking into it, though, I found that unless you're really good, there's just no money in it. So I've decided to keep music as a hobby and go into something with more of a future, which gives me loads of opportunities for getting to the top – so I'm going to study medicine.

Speaker 4: I was pretty rebellious when I was young – I hated school and never wanted to conform to anything. I had these grand ideas of travelling round the world. I was positive I'd never settle down to an office job – I was going to make my fortune, though I wasn't sure how – I just knew it'd be something I'd enjoy. Then I began to see sense, and started taking an interest in lessons – my parents ran their own business and they talked to me about what they did. It seemed pretty interesting so it wasn't long before I realised I wanted to do the same. I guess I'll come across lots of different people, too.

Speaker 5: Funnily enough, I've always been a home person – I love hanging out with the family and chilling with friends. I've got loads of hobbies, and we never went on exotic holidays as a family. Then I got interested in languages at school and found I was pretty good at them – but it's not much good understanding different languages if you don't use them, is it? So what I'm thinking of doing is going into the travel business – and I'm realising just how much of the world I want to see! It's very exciting. My friends are rather envious, actually!

Unit 9, Listening Activity 1

Track 18

Interviewer: We're talking to Carol Johnson, a successful young cyclist with big ambitions. Carol, tell us how it all started.

Carol: Mum's a nurse, dad's a solicitor, my sister's into music – no sport at all at home! I remember going round to a friend's house when I was six. I couldn't ride a bike but she could – and so could her four-year-old brother! I hated that! My friend's dad helped me and eventually I managed to ride it. I pestered my parents to buy me a cheap second-hand bike and from that moment I was completely hooked – I rode it everywhere. It wasn't until I went to university to study sports science that I took up cycling competitively.

Interviewer: What kind of person are you?

Carol: I'm very competitive – my sister got irritated when I turned everything into a contest. But I don't understand athletes who boast about what they're going to achieve. You're better off keeping your mouth shut, training as hard as possible and when it comes to the day, doing all your talking on the track – that's my way. I try to unleash my drive in training and my competitive spirit in races. When I'm racing, I'm not the same person.

Interviewer: How do you feel about training?

Carol: I wouldn't dream of missing a session. It may be the worst pain imaginable but you either do it a hundred percent or you don't do it at all – that's what makes the difference between you and others. You can give ninety-nine percent and the coach wouldn't know – but you would. It's being able to give everything, every day, so if you get beaten, you accept it because you've done your best. You get out what you put in. If you really work hard at something, you can achieve anything.

Interviewer: Are sportspeople arrogant or just confident in general?

Carol: It's a misconception that they're arrogant – it's self-doubt that drives them because if you believed you were going to win all the time, that it was easy, why bother? Every day you're unsure about your fitness, your injury status. It's how you deal with those concerns, particularly on race day – that's the key. You have to be quite selfish as an athlete and I suppose that comes across as arrogance sometimes. But I don't race for second place.

Interviewer: How do you feel about luck as part of success?

Carol: Athletes can be lucky with their bodies and injuries but it's about ambition and determination, not only luck. If I think about the consequences of losing, I perform badly – it's not exactly fear of failure but fear of having sacrificed everything for nothing. When negative thoughts pop into my head I keep them out by visualising the race, what I want to happen. Lots of athletes do that before the start. The more you rehearse, the more it seems natural it will happen that way – is that simply luck?

Interviewer: Do you enjoy the media attention?

Carol: I try to handle journalists and photographers as I want to be treated myself. They're doing their job just like me. It's hard when you've just lost and you want to go and hide but you still have to do interviews and show up for sponsor events. I know that without financial backup I couldn't do it, so I try to focus on what's important and not let other things bother me. And I don't complain when I win and everyone wants to interview me!

Interviewer: What advice would you give other young cyclists?

Carol: When I won my first big medal, I realised it changes nothing. It was just part of my life, not everything. It's about balance, and I'm aware of the dangers of success – sometimes achieving your goals can bring elation, then depression and a loss of focus. Make sure you feel the excitement because it doesn't go on for long. and all the money and success in the world won't be worth it if you hate what you're doing. You'll have to move on to other things as you get older anyway.

Interviewer: Thanks for talking to us, Carol …

Unit 9, Speaking Activity 2

Track 19

Interlocutor: Do you think luck is important in life?

David: OK. Let me see. Well, I always wish my friends good luck before an exam or job interview so I suppose that does mean I believe in it to some extent. What about you?

Sara: Me too – and I really believe it makes a difference. I always carry a – I'm not sure how to say this in English – it's a little thing that is supposed to be lucky. It's a silver bead that my grandmother gave me. If I did an exam without it, I know I would fail.

David: Do you mean that you actually think it affects your success in the exam?

Sara: Well, yes. I do.

David: Well, I suppose I do too now I come to think of it. I have things I always do like wearing the same socks and walking on the same side of the street on the way to the exam.

Interlocutor: How much does luck contribute to success in sporting events?

David: Well, it's difficult to say but not so much, in my opinion. I mean other things are more important like er, – I can't remember the word – how well you can do things like hit the ball or passing in football.

Sara: But in tennis, for example, you often see that for one player the ball hits the top of the – what's it called? – you know, the long thing that divides the court into two halves – and the ball doesn't go over. That's to do with luck if you ask me.

David: So you think luck is more important?

Sara: No, not always. What I meant was that in some sports it can play quite an important role. I'm very superstitious. There are a lot of things that I avoid doing, like stepping on the lines on the pavement or walking under those things that you use to climb up to paint the house – and if I do, my English friends tell me to say 'bread and butter'!

David: Why?

Sara: Well, as far as I know, it's supposed to stop anything terrible happening to you.

David: But perhaps some superstitions are logical.

Sara: What do you mean?

David: What I'm trying to say is that sometimes there really is a danger. For example, the painter could drop something and it could fall on you and cause some kind of harm or damage to you physically.

Interlocutor: Do superstitions ever stop people doing things they might enjoy or benefit from?

David: I'm sorry, did you say enjoy?

Interlocutor: Yes.

David: Right. I suppose they do but I would never decide not to go on a trip or something because it was on the thirteenth of the month.

Sara: So what you're saying is that if you go to the airport and the airline gave you seat 13D on the plane, you would still go?

David: Well, I might feel a bit … not exactly afraid but kind of a bit worried and uncomfortable but it wouldn't stop me flying.

Unit 10, Listening Activity 1

Track 20

Speaker 1: I think I have lots of friends, though in a way they're more acquaintances I suppose – I don't feel I can share my real innermost thoughts with them. It's not that I don't trust them, because on the whole I do – and I see them every day at school – it's more that I love sport and they don't, which makes it difficult for us to do things together. I regret that a lot and I feel quite jealous when I see groups of friends out together doing stuff. Maybe things will change as we get older and get other opportunities to try new things.

Speaker 2: My closest friend doesn't live near me anymore, so we have to keep in touch by phone and email. That's fine – we've known each other since school and our friendship is very deep. I don't think we're really alike – and that's what makes our friendship so interesting – we can tell each other about things we've done which stops us getting bored! We love pulling one another's legs – she's the only one who really gets my jokes – so even though we're very different in other ways that's what keeps us together. As a bonus, we both hate sport, so I don't get dragged to watch football matches!

Speaker 3: We don't see each other very often now even though we both still live in the same town and grew up together. I think we've just grown apart and developed different interests – what's missing for me now is the feeling that I can go to him if I need help – I'm not sure that he'd be there for me. I think that's such a key thing in a friendship. Of course, I miss the fun we used to have, and we always used to play football together, but I've got other friends to do stuff with, and you just have to laugh about it and move on.

Speaker 4: I often read those quizzes in magazines – you know, 'Are You a Good Friend' – that type of thing – I usually come out of them quite well cos I think I'm quite sensitive. But what I know about myself is I need to have my friends around me – I'm a people person – and even though there's always social media that's no real substitute. It's not that important to be the same kind of person, nor to like the same kind of things – my closest mates are into very different stuff, though they never hold that against me. We can have a laugh about it, actually!

Speaker 5: Most of my friends like loads of different things – and it's great that we can give ourselves space and not worry about being in one another's pockets all the time. We always have a good laugh together – though not all my mates get my idea of a joke, and they always tell me that truthfully which can be annoying! But we all have the same values, we're the same kind of people really. That's what supports a good friendship, not the other stuff – and if we don't meet up for a few days that's not a problem. We just pick up exactly where we left off!

Unit 10, Speaking Activity 1

Track 21

Here are some things that friends often think are important and a question for you to discuss. Talk to each other about whether these things are really necessary in a good friendship.

Unit 11, Listening Activity 1

Track 22

1

N: You hear two friends talking about a newspaper article about a dog.

M: That article was pretty funny – the one about the dog that skateboards!

F: I'm not sure about that – when you actually think about it, a dog whizzing round the street on a skateboard – ridiculous! It could get in people's way. I'm sure it makes children laugh, though! And it's certainly not something you see every day.

M: Some people reckon it's not worth writing about – it's just not connected to anything useful. I suppose they could be right.

F: There are more meaningful stories to put in the paper – though it's not bad to have it exactly, it's just out of touch with what's important.

M: Well, it made me smile anyway.

2

N: You hear a voicemail message a woman has left on your phone.

F: I'm calling from Q3 telephone services. Are you aware of some of our new special rates for international calls? Whatever you're currently paying on your existing deal we guarantee you'll find our rates competitive and we're confident you'll make substantial savings on your monthly bills. This opportunity will only be available for a short time, so why not take us up during the trial period? Call us on 0294 68500 to talk it through, or go onto our website, which sets out all the details. It's all very clear, and as you've been a customer of ours in the past you can take full advantage of this deal. Thanks for your time.

3

N: You hear two friends talking about shopping for clothes.

F: Loads of shops sell fake designer branded clothes. But if they're reasonable quality, does it matter if they're not the real thing?

M: You can tell fake gear a mile off. I'd rather buy fewer clothes even though I know designer stuff's over-priced than buy too much cheap stuff.

F: I think it's exploitation – but I don't want to stand out in something that's out of date. My friends would laugh at me!

M: If you can get hold of designer clothes with a slight fault – like a small hole – they're much cheaper.

F: That's such a hassle – and I hate mending, anyway!

M: Then you're stuck!

4

N: You overhear a man leaving a voicemail message.

M: Hi Pete. I don't think I'll get away before five after all, so there's no chance of being able to eat with you before the film – it's a good thing we hadn't booked in anywhere! I'll probably stop off and get a sandwich on the way and catch up with you at the box office, but you go ahead and get something yourself – there's that café opposite the cinema though I've no idea what it's like. According to the radio there's loads of traffic building up on the motorway so I might get held up – if that happens, I'll call you so you can buy the tickets for us both. See you soon!

5

N: You hear two friends talking about a concert they've just been to.

M: Well, that was quite an experience!

F: It certainly was – the stadium was magnificent, though the way the seating was set out meant that I couldn't always see the big screens on the left.

M: It was a bit weird, I agree. But it didn't seem to spoil anyone's enjoyment.

F: True – everyone was singing and dancing all the way through – not that I was tempted to do that – I just wanted to hear the band! Actually, I've never seen such amazing lighting and special effects, though – they were a total knockout. If only everything else had been perfect …

M: You can't have everything …

6

N: You hear part of an interview with a young dancer.

M: Jennie, you've just left ballet school and joined a professional company. How's that going?

F: I'm so lucky to have got a contract when I've only just left school. The daily routine is similar to school, which is comforting – of course the standard is a lot higher and you're expected to keep practising and improving all the time which is tough. I was afraid that the older dancers would ignore me – you know, the newbie! – but they've really been there for me. I'm looking forward to the first performance on stage – I haven't got a big part, but at least I'm there and I love all the rehearsing involved.

7

N: You hear a young man talking about his first experience of rock climbing.

M: I was persuaded to have a go by my mates, and I was attracted by the whole physical aspect of it – I love a challenge. I knew that I had good balance and things like that so I wasn't too bothered about the potential risks. There are so many safety checks that you can't really go wrong! We were only climbing up a small cliff, and I felt a bit silly at first – the others were so much better than me – and annoyingly it started raining so the rock face got rather slippery. That was an unexpected hazard, though no-one seemed to mind. I'll definitely go again.

8

N: You hear two people talking about a new leisure centre.

F: The new leisure centre has got off to a good start – loads of interesting things on offer.

M: I like the look of the classes – a pity they're pricey, but I guess they'll be popular.

F: I really enjoyed the one I tried.

M: They do seem to have catered for everyone, particularly the lower age group – that's really good. It'll encourage a healthy lifestyle.

F: The swimming pool's great – and it's open into the evening.

M: I wonder whether people who live nearby will be happy about that – it might have been wise to only open during the day at first.

F: I'm sure everyone will accept it – it's such a great facility.

Unit 11, Speaking Activity 1

Track 23

Interlocutor: In this part of the test I'm going to give each of you two photographs. I'd like you to talk about your photographs on your own for about a minute and also to answer a short question about your partner's photographs. It's your turn first. Here are your two photographs. They show people on trips in remote regions. I'd like you to compare the photographs and say why you think the people are going on a trip in a remote region.

Candidate: Both these photographs show people on expeditions. In the first photograph there is a group of people. I'm not sure exactly where they are but it could be the North Pole or somewhere like that because they're all wearing very warm outdoor clothing and there's a lot of snow on the ground. The people are all carrying heavy backpacks and are dragging big bags that might have tents or some other kind of equipment in them. In some ways the second photograph is similar because again we see someone in a very isolated part of the world. Like the people in the first photograph, this person seems to be very warmly dressed and we can see some snow on the mountains in the background, so presumably it's very cold. The main difference is that this person is alone, or at least we can't see anyone else in the photograph. Also he's travelling by bicycle, whereas the people in the other photograph were travelling on foot. It could be somewhere like the Himalayas or the Andes but I'm not really sure. I think the people in both photographs must have gone on their trip to have new experiences, and to face new challenges – maybe they wanted to see how well they could manage in difficult conditions.

Unit 12, Listening Activity 2

Track 24

Hello, I'm Carrie, and it's great to be here and share my experiences of writing crime novels with you. I've been writing novels for ten years now. What do you imagine a writer's life is like? Do I sit for hours in my own world waiting for inspiration to strike and then dash off words at a furious rate? Definitely not! Writing isn't a random activity but a skill, which in theory anyone can master, but the reality is it's hard work, especially those times when your mind is completely empty – just like your computer screen! That's what's generally known as writer's block but I like to call it a nightmare! So, now I'd like to pass on a few tips that helped me along the way. Before deciding to write a book, think about why you want to do it. Some people expect huge financial rewards but there are no guarantees of success and there are safer ways to make a fortune. Others want to be famous so you must identify your own motivation first. I believe that people wanted to read what I had to say and I could tell a good story. That sounds like the best reason, but it may not be enough to keep everyone going in difficult times. Simply wanting to do it is not enough. You have to know how to write for the market. Crime is the number one best-selling genre in the world and you must do your research. I spent ages finding out about the way various police departments work, especially their systems and so on. Identify what readers want. What I did was get hold of books by best-selling authors and analyse them chapter by chapter, line by line. That told me the main reason for their high sales figures and what makes them special. If you're planning to write crime fiction you really need to understand what people enjoy about it. That helped me, but it's pretty complex. We're all competitive – we want to be better than everyone else, and one of the ways we can do this is being the first to solve a mystery. Take crosswords for instance – finishing one gives a feeling of satisfaction and pride. People love them and that's why crime fiction is popular too. Readers want to go through the clues and guess the identity of the murderer before the last page. What about the practicalities of writing? The best piece of advice I was given was to remember that crime writing has rules and conventions, and to follow them. On a personal level I also learnt very early that I shouldn't try to improve things while I'm writing – that slows me down. I have to finish the whole story before I go back and concentrate on details, though I know everyone's different. But you do have to work closely with an editor and listen to their advice rather than just your friends or family. I find it hard to know when to stop but if you keep adding too many details they can interfere with the narrative, and make the plot difficult to follow. Don't imagine you can relax when you've written the book – you still have to make sure it sells. There's the back cover of your book with the synopsis of your novel to do. It needs to be short but it must grab the reader's attention. So show your summary to friends – would it make them want to read the book? New writers don't realise that you also have to be quite good at marketing. I've had to do a lot of promotional work, including making personal appearances and signing copies – I don't enjoy that but it's part of the job. I think I've been so lucky – I can't imagine wanting to do anything else, even though it is more difficult than you might think! So now – have I covered everything?

Practice test, Listening Part 1

Track 25

Extract 1

Oh, hello, it's Sara Jones here. I've got two tickets for this evening's show, but unfortunately I'm not very well and won't be able to make it. I know you don't give a refund unless you can resell them, but would it be possible for me to come next Saturday instead? I'm quite prepared to pay any admin fee and I don't mind which part of the theatre the seats are in – even the restricted view would be OK. The problem is I can't get the tickets back to you today. Could you call me on 786533 when you get this message, so I can give you the details? Many thanks.

Extract 2

M: Well, that was a load of hype! I really thought it'd be brilliant after all the trailers.

F: Bits of it were! The technical side for instance – I've never seen anything like it – it all looked so realistic to me.

M: Hm, I found it all a bit of a bore really. The only thing for me was the performance of the stars – they made it something to remember.

F: Hm, I was particularly moved by the young girl's scenes – it was her first film, wasn't it? She's so talented – we'll be seeing a lot of her in the future.

M: Hopefully not in films like this one!

Extract 3

M: I can't believe I'm still hanging round – I checked in ages ago! I don't normally have problems with this carrier – that's why I fly with them on business.

F: I've been waiting since ten! A friend's meeting me at the other end – she'll be really fed up!

M: It could be a problem with the incoming flight – bad weather conditions or something – but they're not exactly keeping us informed, are they? It'd make it easier if we knew what was happening.

F: I tried asking at the information desk but that didn't get me very far.

M: Well, if it takes much longer I'm going to see if I can change my ticket for another flight.

Extract 4

Hi, Jo – well, I got through the first semester but I'm not sure how! I knew it would be demanding – after all, I've never done anything like it before. I'm enjoying the challenge of the coursework and keeping up with the lectures, though some of it isn't exactly fascinating – I think it's the way the tutors deliver it rather than the subject itself, though. It's not the way I thought it would be, and it takes ages to get everything right – I don't mind putting in the hours but I know you're all a bit annoyed I can't go out as much as before! Next term should be better.

Extract 5

M: Do you like those game shows where people have to do extreme sports to win prizes? They're getting a bit silly, I think.

F: Some of the things they do are totally stupid – whoever dreams up the ideas must have a great sense of humour.

M: There was that one in the swimming pool with enormous red balls they had to run across – it wasn't people falling into the water that made me laugh but the fact that they bounced!

F: What must it cost to put on a game show? I can't imagine how television companies afford it.

M: I guess it's the adverts that pay for it – it probably doesn't cost the TV company much.

Extract 6

It was always my first love – my mother talks about how I'd sing endlessly even when I was very young. At school I hated music lessons, not 'cos of the subject but 'cos it was done in such a boring way! My teachers were pretty annoyed with me, because they realised I was wasting my talent. I went in for a music competition when I was sixteen, which I didn't win, but it got me in touch with like-minded musicians. Now I've joined the band I have to go along with their choice of music, though, which has to be what works commercially, not what I'd choose myself. Once I've really made it things will be very different!

Extract 7

People have enjoyed chewing natural products like bark and tree resin for thousands of years, and such products were often believed to have medicinal properties. Now it is produced commercially in a vast industry with worldwide sales measured in billions of pounds. Although it is so widely used and there are a huge range of different forms of the product, including sugar-free and medicated gum, we're increasingly concerned about the environmental impact of the way people dispose of their gum. The cost of removing it from the streets is enormous, and some wildlife can be seriously harmed by eating it.

Extract 8

I'm pretty fed up with everything I've been hearing over the last few minutes. The people you are talking to seem to be just ringing in to moan and OK, they're taking the chance to say what they think – but they're all so critical. I know giving the opportunity to hear different opinions is the focus of a phone-in programme so if you changed the format it would become pretty pointless, but there seems to be little balance in what you're doing at the moment. I want to make the point that this kind of show should present a range of opinions, not just the negative views as it does now.

Practice test, Listening Part 2

Track 26

Hello, everybody – I'm Anne. I'm here to tell you about the work I do in the film industry, and give you some tips on how to get into it yourselves. I followed a popular route into working behind the scenes by becoming a runner – it's a very junior job but it can lead into any area of film making, from camera work to research to directing. My ultimate aim is to be a producer. It's a rather strange name for a job, and in fact it's a difficult job to define, but you may have noticed it on the credits that come up on the cinema screen at the end of a film. Being a runner involves helping out on the production of a film with what's often referred to as 'odd jobs' but I prefer to call general tasks. I suppose it comes from the idea of running from one job to another! What I actually do varies depending on the film and the location, but I often help members of the production team with things like unpacking the gear, setting up for the shoot and getting food and drinks for the crew – though strangely what I seemed to spend most of my time doing on my very first assignment was photocopying! A runner is really useful when things go wrong, because they can spend time away from the shoot sorting out problems while the film crew and the actors get on with their work. That's the part of the job I like best and no two days are the same. One day I was amused to be asked to go to another town to pick up some equipment that had actually been left behind! No matter how much planning has been done by the production team things can always change at the last minute. What I've found most useful apart from following the director was working closely with the technical crew. From the practical point of view that was brilliant. I learnt loads of really useful stuff, and lots of runners I know have gone on to become camera assistants.

There are certain qualities that make a good runner. Determination is quite important because it is so hard to break into the industry, and it's good if you are energetic, enthusiastic and patient – but it's most important to be what I call a good 'ideas' person. I also learnt never to be late on the first day of a film shoot – it's the worst thing you can do, so you soon learn to be organised. You also meet people from many different backgrounds, so it's vital to have good communication skills.

When you're looking for work, one strategy is to send your details to loads of companies, in the hope of getting a job interview. The biggest problem is that most vacancies aren't advertised in the newspapers – you find out about them through word of mouth, and most of them are only short contracts with small salaries. I've put my CV on several media websites so companies can contact me when they are looking for runners.

People ask me if working as a runner is better than doing a course at college if you want to work in films. At the end of the day, the experience is fantastic but you do also need to have done the groundwork. I think many people who work as runners are attracted by the idea of making contacts that might lead to further opportunities but of course that's not guaranteed.

I have to say that working on any production is exciting because everyone is focused and dedicated to making it work. There is a really strong sense of teamwork which for me is something that is the best part of working in the industry. I love it!

So now – are there any questions?

Practice test, Listening Part 3
Track 27

Speaker 1: I often have problems getting my message across. Some people seem to be natural communicators while others struggle. I find it hard to focus and not beat around the bush – that can be confusing for the listeners, though my slides are good. People have very short attention spans, so you can't include too much redundant stuff like jokes – it's crucial not to stick rigidly to your notes but change things as you go if the audience doesn't get it. Of course it helps to appear credible and some people say the way you stand or move is the thing to concentrate on but I don't agree.

Speaker 2: This may seem obvious to you but it's amazing how many people behave unnaturally to impress others. I was guilty of this myself when I started out because I felt huge pressure to make a good impression on everyone else. But in the long run it didn't work – people see through you. It doesn't matter how good your speaking voice is, or how much of an actor you are, you have to speak from your heart. But nowadays, without being able to use slides effectively you may not be as effective as you could be, though you have to retain your integrity.

Speaker 3: Some people are very animated when they're giving a presentation – they use lots of hand movements and different facial expressions. If this is your style, that's great! If not, don't worry about it. You have to find a way of expressing yourself that you're comfortable with and stick with it. As long as you're getting your views across, which means articulating your words well and not mumbling, that's the key – and if you can make sure everyone in the audience thinks that you are looking at them and talking directly to them, then that's a bonus.

Speaker 4: When I'm passionate about something I tend to speak really fast, wave my arms around and try and get all of the words out at once. When you speak like that and have a lot to say, it's hard for all the information to be processed by the listeners at the end of it. But you need to support what you're saying, so mastering the computer is something I think should come first. The slides can actually slow your speaking down, which is no bad thing – you can write up the key words on the slides, and point them out as you go!

Speaker 5 People used to say I smiled too much – though I don't really get that! But seriously smiling did and still does have a very positive effect on others. It makes your face light up and people can hear it in your voice. Good communication is always made better if people enjoy listening to you. But there's something I learnt very early that for me is the number one tip – if you look away from your audience and have a miserable face, you'll find that people don't warm to you, or worse still, don't trust you. Slick computer skills or jolly jokes can't make up for that!

Practice test, Listening Part 4
Track 28

Interviewer: Kris, you started tennis very young – how did that happen?

Kris: My parents worked at a leisure complex – dad was a tennis coach. I began playing with him when I was four. At my first school I tried rugby which I actually liked better because I could play with my friends, so keeping on going with tennis was really tough. After one rugby match I went home with a cut on my forehead and my parents told me to give it up. Up until then I played tennis twice a week, but after that I played more often and improved rapidly. That got me hooked and by the time I was twelve I was pretty good.

Interviewer: Were you a good student at school?

Kris: I enjoyed school on the whole and I wasn't bad academically, though I couldn't really see the point of it – I already knew what I was going to do. I still keep in touch occasionally with a few old classmates, though my life is very different from most of theirs – but I am grateful for the teachers who taught me that if you dedicate yourself to something, there's nothing that can't be achieved. I started competing seriously when I was fifteen.

Interviewer: You were successful in national tournaments very quickly. How were those early years?

Kris: I fell in love with the buzz of competition. Now the trend is for junior players to go to college first, take a few more years to grow up before trying to make it as a professional but I'm glad I didn't take that route. I just wanted to play, and I was lucky I was tall and strong enough to compete with older players quite easily, though some of them resented me. It taught me a lot about people, and I needed to mature faster – that's given me an edge.

Interviewer: Tell us about your exercise routine and diet on a normal day.

Kris: I try to follow a healthy lifestyle. It's important to avoid stuff like fast food, though I admit I really missed it at first! I train hard – my coach pushes me to build up my strength and stamina. I run first thing every day, then spend four hours working with him on my technique on the court. That's the bit I enjoy, though I know the rest of it is probably even more important. He's introduced me to yoga, which is good for my flexibility – it's hard, though, and I try to avoid it. I don't enjoy the fact that it isn't competitive – I need that to spur me on, though I don't really mind being told what to do.

Interviewer: What do you like most about being a professional?

Kris: Of course it's great seeing places I wouldn't otherwise have the chance to visit – some tournaments take place in fascinating cities, and I always try to look round if I can. Spending so much time away from my family and friends isn't great, though, and hotel rooms are very lonely even when you're earning enough to do what you like. I find it a privilege to talk to loads of interesting people – it's something I never imagined I'd enjoy, but in fact that's what makes it really special.

Interviewer: Do you have any advice for young players who'd like to follow in your footsteps?

Kris: I believe setting goals and working as hard as you can for them is a big thing, though that's not something you can rush. Don't totally ignore those who want to help you – I was rather stubborn at times, and that didn't always make my life easy – though you know yourself best and sometimes you do have to stand up for yourself. Top of the list is how you feel – never underestimate how having a good time builds the real foundation for success.

Interviewer: Finally, is there anything you'd like to achieve?

Kris: Apart from winning that really big tournament?! Many players want to coach, though I don't have the patience or selflessness for that. I'm attracted to the idea of taking up something completely different – say cycling – and getting to the top in that. The idea of becoming a television commentator has crossed my mind – it's glamorous, though probably harder than it looks!

Interviewer: Thanks for your time, Kris …

Practice test, Speaking Part 1

Track 29

Where are you from?

Do you use the internet much in your free time?

Tell us about a television programme you've enjoyed recently.

What's your favourite month of the year?

What do you enjoy most about learning English?

What sort of job would you like to do in the future?

Practice test, Speaking Part 2

Track 30

In this part of the test, I'm going to give each of you two photographs. I'd like you to talk about your photographs on your own for about a minute, and also to answer a question about your partner's photographs. Candidate A, it's your turn first. Here are your photographs. They show people learning to do different things. I'd like you to compare the photographs, and say what you think the people are enjoying about learning to do these different things.

All right?

Thank you.

Candidate B, who do you think is finding learning the easiest?

Thank you.

Now, Candidate B, here are your photographs. They show people sharing an important moment together. I'd like you to compare the photographs and say why you think this moment is important to the people.

All right?

Thank you.

Candidate A, who do you think is enjoying the moment the most?

Thank you.

Practice test, Speaking Part 3

Track 31

Now, I'd like you to talk about something together for about two minutes. Some people think it's necessary to use technology every day, and other people disagree. Here are some things they think about and a question for you to discuss. First you have some time to look at the task.

Now talk to each other about whether it's really necessary to use technology every day.

Thank you.

Now you have about a minute to decide which type of technology does not need to be used every day.

Thank you.

Practice test, Speaking Part 4

Track 32

Which aspect of technology do you think is the least useful?

Some people dislike using technology at all. Why do you think this is?

Why do you think some people always want to have the newest gadgets?

Do you think using a computer always saves time, or does it sometimes waste time?

What do you think is the future for newspapers and magazines that are not online?

Some people say life would be easier and more enjoyable without technology. What do you think?

Pearson Education Limited
KAO Two, KAO Park, Harlow,
Essex, CM17 9NA, England
and Associated Companies throughout the world

www.pearsonELT.com/gold

© Pearson Education Limited 2018

The right of Sally Burgess and Jacky Newbrook to be identified as
authors of this Work has been asserted by them in accordance with the
Copyright, Designs and Patents Act, 1988.

New Edition first published 2018
Twelfth impression 2024

ISBN: 978-1-292-20223-5 (Gold First New Edition Exam Maximiser)
ISBN: 978-1-292-20224-2 (Gold First New Edition Exam Maximiser with Key)

Set in Frutiger Neue LT Pro Thin
Printed in Slovakia by Neografia

Acknowledgements
We are grateful to the following for permission to reproduce
copyright material:

Text
Page 007–008: "How many songwriters does it take to change a chorus?"
By Neil McCormick © Telegraph Media Group Limited 2015; Page 009:
"Talking about music is like dancing about architecture" By Tom Gunn
(www.seasideman.com); Page 013: "Gossip is good for you" By Diana
Hutchinson, 3 Dec 2003, *The Lady* Magazine; Page 013–014: "Identical
twins reunited after 35 years" by Alex Spillins © Telegraph Media Group
Limited 2007; Page 015: "The child stars of the West End" by Sally
Williams © Telegraph Media Group Limited 201; Page 022–023: "Why
not join a rock choir?" By Adrian Monti © Telegraph Media Group Limited
2016; Page 026–027 "North Pole Swimmer's Unique Body Heat Trick"
By Auslan Cramb © Telegraph Media Group Limited 2007; Page 028:
Preparing for the expedition By Cassandra Brooks, used with permission
from Exploratorium Ice Stories, NSF Award # 0733048; Page 036–037:
"Is powdered food the future – Huel put to the test" By Abigail Butcher
© Telegraph Media Group Limited 2016; Page 042–043: "Life as a film
extra: Hollywood's least powerful" By Richard Johnson © Telegraph
Media Group Limited 2009; Page 062–063: "Be lucky – it's an easy skill
to learn" By Richard Wiseman © Telegraph Media Group Limited 2003;
Page 070–071: "How to lose friends" By Hannah Pool, 27 November
2010, Copyright Guardian News & Media Ltd 2017; Page 075: "How do
you measure up as a friend?" By Louise Atkinson; Page 076–077: "A short
hop to Paris" By Emma John, 21 February 2010 Copyright Guardian News
& Media Ltd 2017; Page 084–085: "How I accidentally stole a bicycle" By
Frederika Whitehead, 6 July 2011 Copyright Guardian News & Media Ltd
2017; Page 100: "Skies of the World" by Leonardo Tarifeño, Aerolineas
Argentina; Page 102: "How to see mountain gorillas" © Telegraph Media
Group Limited 2015; Page 111: "How to be a good communicator"
By Carly Taylor, April 2010. http://www.carlytaylor.co

Photos
The publisher would like to thank the following for their kind permission
to reproduce their photographs:

(Key: b-bottom; c-centre; l-left; r-right; t-top)

123RF.com: Duncan Cook Drummond 48bl; **Alamy Stock Photo:** "Ben
Hur" 1959 / MGM / INTERFOTO 43bl, Cultura Creative (RF) 22cl, Myles
Wright / Zuma Press Inc 7tr, ONTHEBIKE.PL 81br; **Getty Images:** Agence
Zoom 110br, Barcroft Media 76bl, Blue Jean Images / Lane Oatey 110cr,
ColorBlind Images / The Image Bank 39tc, DAJ / amana images 36tr,
Dougberry 110tr, George Shelley / Corbis 50br, Juice Images 110bl, Mel
Svenson / Photodisc 39tr, Paul A. Souders / Corbis Documentary 80bc,
PM Images / Iconica 63br, Image Source 22c, Tim Platt / Iconica 29br;
Pearson Education Ltd: Gareth Boden 35br; **Press Association Images:**
Philip Toscano / PA Archive 26bl; **Shutterstock.com:** Africa Studio 82cl,
AniaFotKam 56br, Brian A Jackson 82bl, Danny Smythe 62bl, Elenamiv
30bl, Hannamariah 34bl, Ibooo7 85tr, itm20 37br, mrkornflakes 14tr,
Rawpixel.com 59br, sunabesyou 12bl, Top Photo Corporation / Rex 50cr

All other images © Pearson Education

Every effort has been made to trace the copyright holders and we
apologise in advance for any unintentional omissions. We would be
pleased to insert the appropriate acknowledgement in any subsequent
edition of this publication.

Illustrated by Oxford Designers & Illustrators Ltd.